# The Rise of Zion

STANDING IN HOLY PLACES

BOOK THREE

# THE RISE OF ZION

## BY CHAD DAYBELL

spring creek
**BOOK COMPANY**
Provo, Utah

ISBN 13:  978-1-932898-95-8
e. 1

Published by:
Spring Creek Book Company
P.O. Box 50355
Provo, Utah 84605-0355

www.springcreekbooks.com

Cover design © Spring Creek Book Company
Cover image © Bowie15 | Dreamstime.com

Printed in the United States of America
Printed on acid-free paper

Library of Congress Cataloging-in-Publication Data available upon request

# Author's Note

⸎

I have enjoyed writing this third volume in the series. The characters still have obstacles to overcome, but the storyline is a bit more lighthearted than the first two novels, and it emphasizes the happy lifestyle that awaits the Saints who stay true to the gospel during the tribulations that were portrayed in the earlier books.

This volume also serves as a bridge between the first two novels and the series' final two novels that will focus on the crucial events that will take place right before and after the Second Coming.

The events in this series are fictional, but in order to maintain a sense of realism as the storyline moves forward into the future, there will be inevitable changes in Church leadership within the novels.

I certainly hope President Thomas S. Monson is with us for many more years, and I can easily picture him as the president of the Church portrayed in the first two volumes of this series when the Saints returned to Jackson County, Missouri. I feel that many of his personality traits are evident in that fictional prophet. However, in this volume, that revered prophet passes on, and a new prophet begins his service as president of the LDS Church.

The curious part about writing this series is that while the leaders of the Church in the novels are fictional, there will indeed be an actual prophet presiding over the Church in New Jerusalem. Based on my belief that the Saints' journey to Missouri isn't many years away, I feel that the future prophet is likely already a member of the First Presidency or the Quorum of the Twelve. It is fun to speculate who that person might be, but we only have to look back to the late 1960s to see a situation where unexpected events brought great changes within the Quorum of the Twelve.

At that time, Spencer W. Kimball was often in poor health and there were several apostles who had more seniority in the quorum than he did. The general speculation among Church members was that Harold B. Lee—with his vigor and youth—would eventually lead the Church and probably serve well into the 1980s.

As the 1970s began, President David O. McKay died, and his successor, Joseph Fielding Smith, also died soon afterward. That meant that Harold B. Lee, as had long been expected, became the Church's president. However, other elderly apostles also passed away during this period, and Spencer W. Kimball suddenly found himself as the President of the Quorum of the Twelve, one step away from becoming the prophet. President Kimball often said that no one was praying more for the health and well-being of President Lee than he was.

But less than two years later, President Lee suddenly passed away. His death seemed untimely, but the Lord was in control. It was time for President Kimball to lead the Church, and his presidency was one of the most dynamic eras in Church history.

I only share that story to emphasize that I have no idea who will lead the Church in New Jerusalem, but I am completely confident that the Lord is carefully orchestrating the Quorum of the Twelve so that the right man will be in position at that time to lead the Church forward. It is my prayer that you have also developed a testimony that the Lord is in charge and that we can follow the living prophet, no matter who that man is.

Thanks again for your encouragement and support for this series.

Chad Daybell
June 2009

# A NEW SOCIETY

⚜

Nearly a year had passed since the memorable dedication in Independence, Missouri of the site for the New Jerusalem Temple. The winter that followed had been quite mild, in contrast to the harsh weather of the previous year that had locked most of the United States in ice. The Lord had now tempered the elements, and the Saints were able to work continuously on building the temple and the establishment of Zion.

Ever since the Saints had arrived in Independence, they had called their growing community by the name of New Jerusalem. In the past few months it had developed into a large-sized city that already encompassed the former Kansas City area and beyond. Any buildings or homes that hadn't been damaged during the civil unrest or the Coalition invasion were being modified as suitable dwellings, although a main task of the Saints was removing or destroying any unwholesome remnants of the previous society— magazines, billboards, and so on.

Out of necessity, during the Coalition invasion the Saints had shared everything they owned, from their food and belongings to their tents and homes. That experience had brought a unity and compassion among the Saints to a level that hadn't existed before. Now that peace had returned, the Church leaders felt the Saints were ready to implement the Law of Consecration in New Jerusalem. This was done on a ward level, with the bishop working closely with each family to determine their specific needs.

Each family that was willing to participate would voluntarily turn over its possessions to the Church, and in return was deeded the rights to a home and the accompanying property. Each family member was also expected to contribute to the community in a meaningful way. This created a situation where everyone essentially had the same standard of living, and there were no poor among them. Even from the beginning every person had enough to eat and a good home to live in. Most Saints felt extremely blessed and happily spent each day helping Zion to grow.

However, despite the lessons that had been learned the previous two years, a small minority of Saints still tried to cling to the enticing idea of accumulating wealth. Their efforts led to a brief period of contention in New Jerusalem as they sought to convince the rest of the Saints that capitalism should be Zion's economic foundation. They weren't able to sway the First Presidency, though, and it was a bittersweet day when several dozen families chose to depart from New Jerusalem to start their own community several hundred miles away, rather than live the Law of Consecration.

Following the defeat of the Coalition forces, the area formerly known as the United States was relatively peaceful. There were still small pockets of people throughout the land that had managed to escape the invaders, and now they lived essentially as tribes in rural areas, without a real form of government. America's largest cities were either abandoned or occupied by lawless gangs.

Meanwhile, the rest of the world was engaged in steady warfare. The alliance between China and Russia had disintegrated into a power struggle, with Russia gaining the upper hand. Their continual battles had disrupted the already-weakened global economy, which had led to a domino effect of distress, hunger, and chaos in countries around the world.

The governments in South America had collapsed, and many Saints living there had felt prompted to leave their temple compounds and travel north to New Jerusalem. The Guatemalan Saints who had been among the first to arrive in Missouri had been busily preparing entire communities on the eastern outskirts of Kansas City for their South American cousins, so when these Saints arrived they were able to easily adjust to life in Zion and the Law of Consecration. One of the blessings of New Jerusalem was that people who had gathered to Zion from across the world were able to maintain their customs, hobbies and traditions within their neighborhoods, while still adhering to the counsel and instructions given by the General Authorities.

During this time, Saints living in Europe and parts of Asia were quietly guided to safety under the direction of their priesthood leaders. Various groups had left their temple sites and made their way to the British Isles, where Church members had refurbished abandoned ships. These ships would depart from the British Isles and cross the Atlantic Ocean, then round the tip of Florida into the Gulf of Mexico. The ships would soon reach New Orleans, where they were met by representatives from Zion, who would record their information and send it along to officials in New Jerusalem so that arrangements could be made for the new arrivals.

New Orleans itself had never fully recovered from the devastation caused by Hurricane Katrina and subsequent storms. Nearly all of the city's residents had finally left for good during the Coalition invasion, but now the city served as a resting place for the Saints as they arrived from across the sea.

After the Saints had rested sufficiently in New Orleans, they would board smaller boats and make the journey north up the Mississippi River, arriving in St. Louis. During the past year the Church had repaired a set of railroad lines across Missouri, and each day several trains made the journey from St. Louis to the western outskirts of New Jerusalem. There the new arrivals were housed in apartment complexes, and if they agreed to live the Law of Consecration, they would soon be assigned a home in a suitable neighborhood with their family and friends within the ever-growing boundaries of New Jerusalem.

Some of the Saints' journeys across the ocean rivaled that of the Jaredites in terms of miracles—and seasickness—but when they finally arrived in Zion, their faces beamed with happiness as they saw the peaceful neighborhoods and the partially completed temple starting to rise above the city.

Once each family was settled into a home, the men and teenage boys and girls were asked to spend their first three months in Zion helping renovate abandoned houses in preparation for the arrival of other Saints, thereby paying for the home they had received with their labor.

The women, meanwhile, were maintaining their households, working in the neighborhood garden, caring for the younger children, and establishing schools. For the most part, the Saints felt constantly cheerful. They focused on doing good deeds, with no real interest in pursuing evil habits.

Over the past year, the three main couples in this series were making their own contributions to the cause of Zion. As this volume begins:

**Tad and Emma North** live in New Jerusalem with their children David, Charles, and Leah. Tad has served continually as a brick mason on the temple site's main plaza since construction began, and he loves every minute of it.

Emma has helped establish their neighborhood garden where she works for four hours a day. She has also been serving as part of a team called by the First Presidency to reestablish the Church's curriculum materials. Her main focus is to assist in updating the Primary manuals for the coming year, adding in stories and examples from the Saints' recent experiences.

**Doug and Becky Dalton** look forward to being reunited again soon. Doug has been away the past year as one of the 144,000 high priests called to seek out faithful Saints and gather them to Zion. He has spent his time working near New York City.

Becky has been caring for their three children this past year. Justin and Heather are attending school, and their toddler Daniel's health problems have subsided somewhat. Many women in the ward have helped care for him, allowing Becky to serve as a teacher for younger children at the elementary school that has been established in their neighborhood.

As New Jerusalem was being organized and certain parts of the city were assigned to incoming groups, **Josh and Kim Brown** chose to live among the thousands of Guatemalan Saints who had become a key part of their lives. It has been a great blessing for the Browns to keep close contact with the friends they had made on their journey to Zion, and the Guatemalan sisters have been wonderful in helping Kim deal with the experience of raising Timothy and Tina, the twins she gave birth to the previous autumn.

There had been several babies born soon after the Saints arrived in Zion, but Timothy and Tina were the first set of twins born in New Jerusalem, and the Saints had showered the new apostle and his little family with small gifts, along with cards and letters of congratulations. The twins were now nearly a year old and crawling all over the place, but as time allowed, Kim spent time serving as a Family History online data coordinator as the Church prepared to reopen several temples that were within a few hundred miles of New Jerusalem and take a major step forward in family history work.

Josh's days were devoted to his assignments as a member of the Quorum of the Twelve Apostles, and each day was filled with inspiring experiences. He felt so grateful for the opportunity to work with his fellow apostles, and he had witnessed firsthand how the Lord was preparing to provide the Saints with blessings and opportunities they could scarcely imagine.

Now on with the story.

# CHAPTER 1

Doug Dalton carefully looked out from the 70th floor of the Empire State Building, high above the abandoned, earthquake-shattered ruins of Manhattan. He peered through an opening where a window had once been and looked across the land for signs of smoke. As one of the 144,000 high priests called to gather good-hearted souls to Zion, he was always on the lookout for anyone. Since a column of smoke often signaled a group of people, Doug would chart the smoke's general location on a map he had found of the New York City area, planning to visit the people at a later time.

The Empire State Building had held up well during these recent years of strife. Constructed during the Great Depression of the 1930s, the building was solid like a fortress, especially compared to the many other skyscrapers around it that had recently tumbled to the ground from either the earthquake or the Coalition's bombs. However, the building hadn't been completely spared. Portions of the top floors had collapsed in the earthquake, including the famed observation deck, so Doug didn't feel safe going much higher inside the building. Besides, after climbing 70 stories of stairs, he decided he could see the surrounding area just fine.

Doug felt much safer at his permanent home several blocks to the north. Soon after arriving in New York City the previous year, he had gone straight to the Manhattan Temple near West 66th Street, not far from the southern end of Central Park. The temple was relatively undamaged from the earthquake, and he had been thrilled to see that large amounts of food had been stored there.

6

Several opened containers of wheat and rice indicated that a few Saints had lived there for a while, but the temple had been empty when he had arrived.

The temple no longer had electricity, but enough light came through the windows to make it a comfortable place to live. Most importantly, Doug felt the Spirit of the Lord more strongly there than in any other location on the East Coast. At times he was certain there were unseen angels at his side. This was comforting, because it had been a lonely year, but the Lord had blessed him in an unusual way. Every few days when he prayed he was granted vivid dreams—almost visions—of his wife and children in New Jerusalem. He was grateful to see Becky enjoying her service as a school teacher, and that his older children Justin and Heather were healthy and happy. He also saw his youngest child, little Daniel, who was always smiling despite his physical handicaps. Doug missed them all so much, but he knew he was on the Lord's errand.

Doug actually spent only a couple of days each week at the temple to restock his food and to record his most recent experiences. The rest of the time he was out in what he called "the wilderness." He came upon that name because he was amazed how quickly nature was beginning to reclaim the countryside. Weeds, shrubs and even small trees were sprouting in areas that had been bustling sidewalks and busy roadways less than two years earlier.

During his first visit to the Manhattan Temple he had found a file cabinet filled with helpful information—the addresses of all the LDS meetinghouses in the temple district—and he had systematically walked to each location. Nearly all of the buildings had been empty, but inside a few meetinghouses he had found small groups of Saints. They were living off their combined food storage and were feeling isolated, because communication with Church headquarters had been cut off at these buildings when the Coalition attack began. Doug had been pleased to see how in most cases the bishop had continued in his role as a shepherd for the Lord's sheep, and that in most cases the Saints had stuck together and stayed true to the gospel.

When Doug would inform these groups of Saints that New Jerusalem had been established, at first they wouldn't believe him, but then they would hug him and weep for joy at the news. Doug would give them instructions on the safest highways to follow on the way to Zion, and he would assist them as they packed up and departed. He also would give them a letter to deliver to Becky and the children so they would know how he was doing.

As the months passed and all of the area meetinghouses had been accounted for, Doug had begun making that strenuous climb up the Empire State Building every couple of weeks, where he would look for the columns of smoke that indicated possible civilized groups. His favorite route from the temple to the building was the 32-block walk along Broadway and through Times Square. The remnants of American society were everywhere on that route, and at times it was still hard for Doug to comprehend that the nation he had grown up in no longer existed.

As a boy, Doug had stayed up late on New Years Eve with his family, watching on TV as Dick Clark would stand on a platform above Times Square and count down to the new year. There had always been more than a million people crammed into the square and the surrounding streets, blowing their noisemakers and creating quite a scene as they waited for the glittering ball to drop.

The crowds and confetti were nowhere to be found, though, on the past December 31st when Doug had walked to Times Square to mark the occasion. What had struck him the most had been the silence. His only companions that day in the heart of New York City were a flock of pigeons and a few rats, and he'd returned to the temple long before darkness had settled in.

As Doug began investigating the locations where columns of smoke were rising, he encountered people living in tribe-like circumstances in broken-down homes, trying to grow food. They would treat him very cautiously, and Doug would approach them with a prayer in his heart. Some groups would shout at him and try to scare him off, in which case he would quickly depart, but most of the people were curious about this stranger who had clean clothes and was well-groomed. They would invite him to meet their leader, and Doug would first explain that he was a Christian missionary. If the people responded favorably—and if the Spirit directed him to—he would stay with them a day or two and teach them gospel principles. Most of the groups seemed content to just live out their lives as they were, but a couple of times Doug felt prompted to tell the group about New Jerusalem and invite them to journey there, where they could join with the Saints and improve their lives both temporally and spiritually.

One day the Spirit prompted Doug to journey many miles west until he reached Pennsylvania. As he passed through the city of Allentown and walked up a small rise in the road, he saw a man standing at the top of the hill about fifty yards ahead.

"Hello there," Doug called out. The man waved and waited for Doug to reach him. As Doug approached, he noticed the man was wearing what could only be termed as Amish clothing.

Doug stuck out his hand. "I'm Doug Dalton, a Christian missionary."

The man took Doug's hand and gave it a firm shake. "I'm Ezekiel. It's good to see another Christian. There aren't too many of us left."

Doug smiled. "You're right. That's why I'm just visiting the countryside and keeping an eye out for good people like yourself."

"You didn't see too many people on your way, did you?"

"Nope, just a few scattered groups," Doug said. He paused for a moment, then added, "I don't mean to pry, but are you Amish?"

"I am," Ezekiel said.

"How are your people doing? Did the Coalition find you?"

Ezekiel shook his head. "Their soldiers came in this direction from Philadelphia and went on to attack Pittsburgh, but they never even noticed us. Why would they? We never received the chip. I'm sure our farms and houses were just a big blank on the Coalition's chip scanners."

Doug laughed. "I'm actually a Mormon, and most of us didn't receive the chip either. We survived just fine, hidden away in the Rocky Mountains."

Doug then filled in Ezekiel on the outcome of the final battle between the Coalition soldiers and the Elders of Israel, and Ezekiel was touched by the news. "My people will certainly be grateful to hear that the Mormons—of all people—have finished off the Coalition."

"Yes, we were somewhat surprised as well," Doug said with a grin. "We're now building a new city in Missouri. You and your people are certainly welcome to join us."

Ezekiel slapped Doug on the back. "Thanks for the offer, but I think we're content right where we are. In fact, life hasn't been this good in a long time."

"I understand," Doug said. "May God bless you."

As Doug bid Ezekiel farewell and began his journey back to Manhattan, he could only shake his head in amazement. It was a strange twist that the two religious groups many Americans had considered backward and out of touch—the Amish and the Mormons—were the ones now prospering in this new world.

❖ ❖ ❖

As Doug returned to Manhattan and peered across the landscape once again from the Empire State Building, he sensed this would be his last time in the skyscraper. There were only a few columns of smoke rising across the land, and he had already visited each of those locations. He had made a valiant effort to reach every person he could find, and the only ones left didn't want anything to do with Zion. It was time to move on.

He walked to a window and looked south to where Wall Street had once been the center of the world's financial markets. Billions of dollars had been traded there daily, but no one was there now. He had spent a day wandering the New York Stock Exchange and saw all of the blank computer screens. In some ways—besides all of the dust—it was like everyone had just turned off their computers, packed up for the day and would return the next morning to continue business as usual.

Doug frowned as he pondered how several of the world's key events in recent years had been sparked right there on the southern tip of Manhattan. First had come the infamous attack on the World Trade Center on September 11, 2001, which led to the prolonged wars in Iraq and Afghanistan.

Another event that had focused attention on Wall Street was the financial trouble in late 2008 that had been known as the home mortgage crisis. The stock market had plunged that October, and there was a general panic among Americans that led to the country's first recession in several years. In response, the federal government had quickly approved billions of dollars for massive corporate bailouts just ahead of the election of U.S. President Barack Obama. His rallying cry of "Yes, we can!" lifted the spirits of the citizens and created much-needed optimism throughout the country. The national media praised his decisions, bringing a sense of change and hope to the United States.

The new president devoted his first months in office to passing additional large stimulus packages while promising to cut the federal deficit. The short-term effects of these efforts—combined with the enthusiasm and charisma of the new president—improved the nation's sense of well-being for a while, but the unrelenting spending by Congress and the "redistribution of wealth" couldn't go on forever without severe repercussions for the nation.

Those effects did eventually come, and the economy never really got rolling again despite the government's efforts. The ever-growing national debt became a major liability, and this debt weakened the United States' standing in the world. Russia and China in particular grew wary of America's lack of economic strength—and they saw the country's overall vulnerability.

Meanwhile, the liberties of America's citizens continued to be curtailed in many ways. Many citizens began to feel like the government controlled every aspect of society. Gradually but assuredly the nation's leaders used legislation and court rulings to move the American economic system from capitalism to a form of socialism. Many companies had been taken over by the federal government either through bankruptcy negotiations or federal loans. Government kept getting bigger and more intrusive, and small businesses began to whither away.

There was a final burst of hope with the introduction of the government-sponsored chip implant. Through the influence of Hollywood celebrities and other media propaganda, the vast majority of Americans chose to "Get the chip." But it was a short-lived euphoria. The nation was already sliding down a slippery slope of civil unrest in many cities due to natural disasters and a devastating series of health concerns, such as influenza outbreaks. These troubles left the United States quite fragile and already on the brink of disaster when the Coalition invasion took place.

Doug shook his head to fight off the bad memories of that era, hardly believing how quickly the United States had evaporated. The stress upon the Saints at that time had been enormous, particularly financially. The economic conditions had forced many faithful Saints to lose their jobs, sell their homes for a loss, file for bankruptcy, or all of the above. These hard times placed an added burden on the Church's bishops and welfare system, but the Lord had provided in many ways for those Saints who stayed true to their covenants.

Unfortunately, many Church members who hadn't been spiritually prepared for the economic troubles gave into fear and made unwise choices that they would later regret, such as receiving the chip.

As difficult as that period of time had been, in retrospect it emphasized to Doug the importance of heeding the words of the prophet. He remembered listening during the General Priesthood Session in 1998 as President Hinckley had spoken about Joseph of Egypt and his dream of seven years of plenty and seven years of famine. President Hinckley had emphasized Joseph's dream again in October 2001 after the World Trade Center attacks, seeming to start the clock ticking on his prophetic warning.

In those talks, President Hinckley had made it clear that he wasn't attempting to outline a specific number of years before those events happened—and in the commotion of world events it really wasn't possible to pinpoint an exact moment when the good times became the bad times—but the underlying problems were certainly clear to everyone by late 2008.

As Doug scanned the horizon and looked at the ruins of New York City below him for a final time, he realized he'd been an eyewitness to the truthfulness of President Hinckley's words. Now he was just thankful the bad times seemed to be coming to an end for most of the Saints, and he hoped as New Jerusalem began to grow, the American continent would again flourish.

Two hours later Doug was back inside the Manhattan Temple, where he knelt humbly and prayed about the next step of his assignment. It was amazing to him how the Spirit had become his constant companion, and at times the voice of the Spirit actually became audible to him, especially when it came to key decisions.

Now, the Spirit spoke once again.

"Your work in this area is complete," the Spirit whispered. "Move south along the Garden State Parkway and travel to the Washington D.C. Temple."

Doug nodded. "I will."

# CHAPTER 2

———— ⚘ ————

Nearly a thousand miles to the southwest, Doug's sister Emma North closed the refrigerator in her home in New Jerusalem as she finished making a snack for her husband Tad. Their family had moved into their new home only a few days earlier, and the smell of new paint still lingered. It was a welcome scent—something that Emma had wondered if she would ever experience again.

For the past several months, Emma's family had been living in an apartment building on the Kansas side of the Missouri River while work crews renovated and upgraded the existing neighborhoods near the site of the New Jerusalem Temple that had been abandoned by their previous occupants who had fled during the Coalition invasion. The Church leaders had said they would gladly return any of the homes to the rightful owners if they ever returned, but after a year no one had ever made such a claim and so the Saints began to move into them as the renovations were completed.

The Norths' new home wasn't large—a modest one-story, three-bedroom house in which their sons David and Charles shared a bedroom, while their daughter Leah had her own room. But it felt like a mansion after where they had lived the past two years—a tent in Hobble Creek Canyon, a crowded home in Manti, and then the cramped apartment in Kansas.

In fact, she and Tad had never been able to quite scrape together enough money to purchase their own home, and now they actually had one, mortgage-free! They didn't even have a utility bill to worry about. The home's power line was part of the city's electrical grid that was connected to the massive new complex of solar panels the Saints had built in western Kansas that took care of all of Zion's energy needs.

Tad and Emma had agreed to live according to the Law of Consecration, the economic system of New Jerusalem. They had consecrated all of their belongings to the Lord, and in return their bishop had assigned them to a home that fit their needs. In all respects, Zion was prospering as the Saints focused on lifting each other up, rather than competing with each other to acquire material possessions. They realized that their trials during the past few years had refined and strengthened them. The new feeling of cooperation transformed their lives and allowed them to more fully serve each other in every aspect.

Emma looked at the clock on the wall and realized she had a few minutes before she needed to meet Tad, so she went to their living room and picked up her acoustic guitar. This was her new hobby. She had played the clarinet when she was a teenager and still could play it decently, but she had always wanted to learn to play the guitar, and now in Zion she had time to do so. In New Jerusalem, everyone was encouraged to develop their talents and interests, and daily life was structured so that people really did have time to learn new skills.

Emma set up her music stand, opened her sheet music and began strumming a new rendition of "How Great Thou Art" that had a 'folk music' feel to it. She had played it for Tad the night before, and he'd really liked it. Now she was adding a few little twists that really sounded nice. After a few minutes of practicing she glanced at the clock again.

"Oops, time to go," she said, and leaned the guitar against the couch. Emma grabbed the bag that held Tad's snack and began walking the few blocks to the temple site where Tad was working to place the final rows of bricks in what was known as The Great Plaza. She rarely went to the work site, but Tad had invited her that day to see how the construction of the temple was coming along. As she walked, she waved to neighbors who were chatting on the sidewalk in front of their well-kept homes. A sense of contentment filled her heart to see how the prophetic vision of Zion was coming to pass.

In reality, the city of New Jerusalem was actually made up of a structured patchwork of mini-communities where all of the Saints' needs were within walking distance of their homes. Small temples called "community temples" were being built in five-mile increments, and a few of them had recently been dedicated, with many more nearing completion. This community layout eliminated the need for automobiles, since even the farthest temple would now be only two and a half miles from home. Some families rode bicycles to travel such distances, but the bikes were mainly used for exercise or entertainment. The Church's scientists had made great strides in solar-powered vehicles, and buses were provided for trips outside the community.

The Church's Temple Ready computer system was back in operation, and the Saints had been able to begin doing temple work for their ancestors again. The thousands of names that had already been approved for temple work at the time of the Coalition invasion had been recovered, and the ordinances for those people were now being completed. For most Saints, however, just the feeling of being in the temple again on a regular basis increased their personal spirituality.

The Spirit was being poured out in even greater abundance within the temples, and the veil between this world and the next became increasingly thin. There were many reports of angelic visits and visions. These experiences often revealed the fate of Saints who had died during the turmoil of the preceding years. Their relatives usually had no way of knowing what had happened to them, but there were occasional reports that spirits were appearing to family members in the temples to explain how they had died and to assure their families they were happy in Paradise. These experiences helped bring closure and peace to many Saints.

As part of the Law of Consecration, each family in Zion was encouraged to have a garden behind their home to supplement their meals, but each neighborhood had a bishop's storehouse that served the same purpose a grocery store did in the previous society. Families could stock up on soups, cereals, bread, and any other food items. The fields and orchards surrounding Zion were producing astounding amounts of fruits and vegetables, and there was more than enough food for everyone.

Very little meat was available during the first year of Zion, due to the lack of poultry and livestock left on the land. Nearly every animal that could be caught had been eaten by the surviving U.S. citizens during the Coalition siege and the horrible winter that followed. However, new flocks and herds had been established by the Saints from a few remaining animals and were multiplying rapidly. This new "Zion" lifestyle, combined with the lean times of the previous two years, meant that the Saints were now healthier than they had been in decades. The stereotype of "overweight Mormons" no longer really applied.

Doctors and dentists cheerfully provided exams to new arrivals, allowing for any health problems or illnesses to be caught early. There were a few hospitals operating, but most of the elderly in Zion preferred to spend their last few days at home with their families, looking forward to rejoining their loved ones in Paradise. Of course, there were occasional accidents that required surgery, and kids were still kids—even in Zion—so stitches were still needed quite regularly.

There were some small issues to resolve as the Saints established their new city. Admittedly, sticking close to home for long periods of time without a vacation had been an adjustment for many of the Saints. For several generations, Americans had enjoyed traveling across the country to such destinations as the Disney theme parks or the national parks, and church leaders recognized the need for the Saints to take an occasional break.

One popular destination was Worlds of Fun, a Kansas City amusement park with roller coasters. The park had survived the invasion nearly intact, and the Saints had cleaned it up and soon had all of the rides operating again. Now each stake was assigned a day every three months that their members could go to the park, traveling there by bus.

Each home was provided a simple computer that could be used for journal writing and family history work. Saints could log into the Church-run internet server that hosted dozens of new wholesome websites that provided instruction and entertainment for all ages.

In fact, wholesome entertainment was blossoming throughout Zion. For example, a rising generation of Osmond boys were reaching teenagehood, and their musical group O3G (Osmond Third Generation) was performing firesides of pop hymns throughout New Jerusalem and stirring the hearts of the daughters of Zion. On a related note, in anticipation of Zion's rapid growth throughout Missouri and into accompanying regions, the Osmond family was given permission to re-establish their musical theaters in the city of Branson with the intention of turning the area into the entertainment capital of Zion.

Family restaurants and playhouses flourished as people who had developed culinary skills or enjoyed the performing arts could continue to cultivate those talents without the financial pressures a business owner faced in the previous society. Families were encouraged by Church leaders to participate in a cultural activity at least once a week, so these establishments received a steady patronage.

The hobby of reading a good book had seemingly been forgotten in the previous era of iPods and cell phones, but in Zion reading was definitely the "in" thing to do again. The Church leaders understood that technology could never replace the experience of snuggling up with an enjoyable novel, and for that reason the publishing division of Deseret Book had been relocated to the Kansas City area.

However, now the company didn't sell books for profit, and there weren't any retail bookstores in Zion. Instead, several new titles in a variety of categories were being published each month, and dozens of copies of each new book were provided to the many neighborhood libraries throughout Zion for the Saints to check out and take home.

Several LDS authors who had been well-known before the Coalition attack continued to write new books, but a new generation of talented writers had emerged in the past year. The most popular books were non-fiction accounts of Saints from all over the world sharing their particular journeys to Zion. The Saints enjoyed reading about the trials and triumphs of their fellow Church members.

Several people who had been in the LDS publishing business prior to the Coalition attack had been assigned by the General Authorities to work on these projects, including Emma's former supervisor at the LDS publishing company she had once worked for. When he discovered she was in New Jerusalem, he immediately requested her assistance. Emma was happy to participate in the editing process of these projects, and she found it to be very rewarding to help prepare these accounts for publication.

In a strange way, the hardest adjustment for Emma was that for the first time in several years she actually felt safe. She had to assure herself that another tragedy wasn't waiting around the corner. This had been a common "ailment" among the Saints members in Zion during the first few months after the war had ended. The newfound sense of peace had been hard getting used to. Many people hadn't fully realized how much stress and depression they had been experiencing. But now that a year had passed since the establishment of Zion, those anxious feelings were becoming mere memories among the Saints.

Emma certainly felt cheerful as she approached the temple plaza. While growing up, she had sometimes heard about the temple the Church would someday build in New Jerusalem, but she had been amazed to see the actual design when it had been released by the First Presidency for the Saints to see. The temple was still only partially completed, but already it was shaping up to be the "Center Point of Zion."

It was becoming clear how the temple would be a complex of 24 buildings arranged in a circular pattern, covering dozens of acres. Each of these buildings alone would be as large as the Provo Temple. From the inside edge of each of these 24 buildings would rise a gold-plated 30-foot-wide arch that would join in the center with the other 23 arches to create an immense dome.

Large glass panels would fill the spaces between the arches, and at the pinnacle of the dome a tall, slender spire would pierce the sky at a height of more than 1,500 feet, making the temple visible for miles around. The 24 "mini-temples" were each magnificent structures in their own right, but the combined effect was mind-boggling. The temple construction area was fenced off and very few of the Saints had been allowed to enter the temple site yet, so Emma felt privileged for the opportunity to see how the construction was progressing.

Tad was waiting for her outside the construction area and as she approached, he handed her a hard hat. "Safety first," he said before greeting her with a kiss. He then guided her through a door that led to the area where he had been working on the plaza. He pointed to the closest mini-temple and said, "As you can see, most of the smaller 24 temples are complete on the outside, but there's still a lot of interior work to be finished."

He led her alongside the building so she could see the area that would become the temple's center atrium beneath the magnificent dome. Teams of workers were welding together pieces for one of the huge circular metal beams that would form part of the dome. Off to the side were large stacks of metal waiting to be assembled. Tad motioned to the pile and said, "The beams are being created in 50-foot lengths in a nearby factory and then brought here to be welded together."

Emma looked at the steel beams. "I thought the plans said the main beams would be made of gold."

"You're right, but they aren't going to be solid gold—they'll be gold-plated," Tad said. "Many of the furnishings inside the temple will also be made of gold."

"That's going to take a lot of gold!" Emma exclaimed as she looked again at the massive beams. "Where will it come from?"

Tad shrugged. "That's a good question, and no one has the answer yet, but we're moving forward in getting the beams ready. We're confident the Lord will provide the gold soon."

# CHAPTER 3

---❧---

Not far from where Tad and Emma stood, Elder Josh Brown looked around the room at his fellow apostles. They were gathered around an oval table in the main conference room of the Church Administration Building, a three-story edifice that was a few blocks from the main temple site. The building had been dedicated as a meeting place for the apostles until the main temple was completed, and although it wasn't a temple, there was a sacred feeling there.

Josh enjoyed his weekly meetings with the First Presidency and the other apostles, but he didn't particularly look forward to the first item on that day's agenda. At the far end of the table stood Dale Turley, once one of the wealthiest men in the world. He had made millions of dollars during his career in the financial world and became somewhat of a "poster boy" for Mormonism, with his face on the covers of many national magazines. He had contributed much of his fortune to the Church prior to the Coalition invasion and was known as a true humanitarian.

In the late 1990s, Dale had built a massive mansion in southern Utah County and had been serving as a stake president at the time of the invasion. He had guided his stake members to a safe refuge deep in the Utah mountains and later led them to New Jerusalem soon after the first groups arrived. His stake members had been absorbed into one of Zion's stakes, and Dale had then been honorably released.

Following his release, Dale and his wife had been willing to live the Law of Consecration and had been assigned to a live in a small two-bedroom home that was built in the 1960s. He had been working for several months as a laborer on a construction crew that was repairing and upgrading several of the office buildings near the temple site, and unfortunately Dale's ego was starting to get the best of him.

Now Dale stood before the apostles and explained that he felt he was being greatly underutilized. The leaders felt sympathetic until he said, "I'm sorry, but I just don't feel happy in that cramped little house. This is supposed to be Zion, and all I do every day is pour concrete and hammer nails."

The prophet stared at him. "Well, Dale, what did you expect? We're building Zion. Did you think it would build itself?"

Dale shrugged, a little embarrassed. "I know, but I must admit I miss the opportunities of capitalism, where you could work hard and really do well for yourself. Here, I can work all day, but I never have anything to show for it. No matter what I do, I'll be stuck in that little house."

The apostles looked at each other, somewhat surprised at the attitude of this man who had served so faithfully in the Church for many years. It demonstrated that while New Jerusalem was a great blessing to the Saints who had been considered part of the lower- or middle-classes in the previous economic system, many of the Saints who had previously been wealthy were now struggling with the dynamics of this new society. Dale was only one of several prominent men the apostles had met with over the past few months who were having trouble humbling themselves.

The prophet's voice rose a little. "Dale, you've made great contributions of your time, talents and money to the Church over the years, but that alone won't earn you exaltation. You need to endure to the end, and right now, your pride has gotten the best of you."

Dale got a bit defensive. "That's not true! I just feel like I've been demoted. I'm stuck working on a crew with a bunch of Guatemalans who don't even know who I am."

Silence filled the room, and a few of the apostles took a quick glance at Josh, who had led those Guatemalans on their treacherous journey to Zion. Dale's comment came across as a sad mix of arrogance and racism. Finally the prophet said, "I love you like a brother, but I'm disappointed in you. Maybe you've been a Mormon all these years, but that last outburst didn't sound like a Latter-day Saint."

Dale hung his head. "I'm sorry. That didn't come out right."

"All we ask is that you do whatever you're assigned," the prophet said. "We all need to pitch in during these first few months. Our past accomplishments are definitely worth remembering, but we've got a former Miss Utah in charge of baking bread for her stake, and a former NFL quarterback assembling wheelchairs for handicapped children, among many other notable people serving where they've been asked. Do you think they feel rich and famous right now? Of course not, but they're doing their assignments without complaint and are loving life."

Dale's face had gone slightly pale. "I realize I'm in the wrong. I apologize for wasting your time."

He started walking toward the door, but the prophet beckoned him to his side. Dale went to the prophet, who put his hand on his arm.

"You're a good man," the prophet said. "Once things settle down, we'll have many positions to fill. We're going to need a lot of temple presidents as we finish up this first round of community temples. Humble yourself, do what is asked, and the Lord will use your skills."

Dale nodded as tears came to his eyes, and a feeling of love filled in the room as he departed. The apostles breathed a collective sigh of relief. In a sense, the hardest part of establishing Zion was over, and the city was beginning to flourish. A group of Saints had just arrived from Australia, and the last apostle that had been overseas was part of that group. So for the first time in many months, all fifteen members of the First Presidency and the Quorum of the Twelve were together once again.

After Dale's departure, Josh looked across the table at the prophet as the apostles discussed other matters, and he couldn't shake the feeling that their beloved leader would soon be leaving them. The prophet had been amazingly resilient during the past two years, and it was clear to everyone that the Lord was sustaining him and helping him accomplish tasks that no other man his age could have done. But in the last few weeks Josh had noticed the prophet becoming more withdrawn and feeble.

Perhaps the prophet also sensed his time on earth would soon come to a close, because he had recently discussed with the apostles his desire to be buried in a small park near the temple site. This had come as a surprise, because in the months since the Saints arrived, they had simply begun maintaining the previously established cemeteries in the area and using the remaining available burial plots.

The park that the prophet had designated wasn't currently a cemetery, but in the past few days one of the Church architects had designed a cemetery grid that contained several hundred burial plots in the center of the park, along with a site for an office.

Josh knew the prophet's passing would come as a shock to most of the Saints. He had become "their prophet" much like other prophets had been to earlier generations, and no one wanted to think of a future without their beloved prophet. Some of the Saints even felt he would live until the Savior's Second Coming, but Josh knew there was still too many prophecies yet to be fulfilled. The time was fast approaching when a new prophet would lead the Saints, and Josh knew that man would lead Zion to even greater heights.

# CHAPTER 4

It had been nearly two weeks since Doug Dalton had departed on foot from Manhattan, and finally the spires of the Washington D.C. Temple were in sight. He had never expected it to take him so long, but the destruction throughout southern New Jersey and the Philadelphia area had been much greater than he had imagined. In some areas the bridges across the rivers had been completely destroyed, and at times he'd been forced to make a small raft out of broken boards to make it across the river and continue his journey.

As Doug approached the main gate to the temple grounds, he was met there by a man holding a shotgun. "What's your purpose here?" the man asked as he positioned himself between Doug and the gate. Doug studied the man and sensed he didn't intend to hurt him. He was simply defending the temple grounds.

"I'm Doug Dalton, one of the 144,000 high priests sent by the apostles to search for the pure in heart. I'm hoping to rest for a couple of days, though, with some fellow Saints."

The man gave him a funny look. "I need to talk to my leader before I let you in."

Doug waved his hand. "I understand. I'll wait here."

The guard locked the gate behind him, but five minutes later the guard hurried back with another man, who called out, "Is that really the legendary Doug Dalton?"

Doug peered through the gate, and his heart leapt as he saw the familiar face of Billy Fox, a friend he had known since their days as teenagers in Springville, Utah.

"Wow, you're a sight for sore eyes," Doug said to Billy. The guard opened the gate and the two friends embraced, then they quickly got caught up on their lives as they walked toward the temple. Billy had finished medical school at George Washington University and had been planning to move back to Utah when the Coalition invasion began. He had gathered with other Saints at the temple grounds, but the group had lost contact with the Church during the invasion, and so they had decided to stay put, rather than risk being killed. There were about 400 Saints living there, and they had survived thanks to a large collection of food that had been stored in the temple's visitors center prior to the attack.

As Doug listened to Billy's story, he asked, "Didn't the temple have a computer connection to Church headquarters?"

"It did at first, but the Coalition forces targeted all of the power stations throughout the entire region and cut off all electricity," Billy said. "We had a generator in the temple, but after a few weeks it died on us, so we haven't heard anything for nearly a year. We've built handcarts using bicycle parts, and we planned to leave a few days ago and start heading toward Nauvoo, but I felt prompted to wait a while longer."

"I'm glad you waited," Doug said. "There's no need to go to Nauvoo. New Jerusalem has been established, and we can lead this group straight there."

For the first time in several months Billy felt genuine hope about the group's future. "I figured that New Jerusalem would be established soon, but we had no idea whether the Coalition was still in control. All I knew is that our spies hadn't seen them in this area for quite a while."

Doug smiled. "You don't have to worry about the Coalition anymore."

That evening Billy organized a meeting inside the temple where Doug told the Saints his experiences of the past year. The group listened in awe as he told them how the Elders of Israel had defeated the Coalition forces. He explained that since he had departed on his assignment before the Saints left Denver for Zion, he hadn't actually seen New Jerusalem. But he testified of the dreams he had received that showed his family there, and he knew the time had come for this group to make the journey to Zion.

Following the meeting Doug spent two hours talking to families who had specific questions about certain cities where their relatives were, and he was able to answer many of their questions, particularly about locations in the western United States. Doug's visit had energized them all, and they were eager to leave for Zion as soon as possible. Eventually they all settled down for a restless night's sleep.

The next morning a young blonde woman approached Doug. He had been introduced to her the night before, and Doug remembered the vibrant look in her eyes.

"You're Phyllis, right?" he asked as he motioned for her to sit at the table where he was eating a plate of pancakes.

"Yes, you have a good memory," she said. "Thanks for sharing your experiences with us last night. I can certainly relate with what you've gone through in New York City."

Doug looked at her curiously. "What do you mean?"

"I know that area well. I used to go to Manhattan with my family every few months."

"Where did you grow up?" Doug asked. "New Jersey?"

"No, I was raised in Baltimore, Maryland," Phyllis said. "My family wasn't LDS, and I've actually only been here at the temple for a few months. I came here alone, and on my way I saw a lot of the destruction you described. I'm happy to say I was baptized soon after I arrived, though."

Doug raised his eyebrows. "Wow, so you spent time out there among the troublemakers? I'd really like to hear your story."

Phyllis smiled. "Well, let me just say I've changed in many ways during the past year. Money and prestige were all that mattered to my parents. We lived in an upper-class neighborhood, and my life seemed great. I was 18, attending college and driving my own sports car. But the Coalition invasion changed everything for us. Thankfully we weren't hit directly during the initial attack, and we stayed tucked away in our home, where my parents had stocked our pantry in case of an emergency. So we had plenty of food to stay alive, but within days the looting mobs moved into our neighborhood."

Phyllis paused to compose herself, wiping away a tear. "One day six men broke down our front door. My dad and brother tried to stop them, but the men stabbed them both to death as I watched from the top of the stairway. The men hadn't seen me, so I ran to my bedroom window, climbed onto the roof and hid behind our chimney. It was safe there, but it was also horrible, because I could hear the dying screams of my mom and little sister echoing from the rooms below. I could also hear the men rummaging through the house, and they soon found our food supply. From their conversations I could tell they planned to stay for several days."

Doug put a comforting hand on Phyllis' arm. "You must have been terrified!"

Phyllis nodded, her eyes now very sad. "It was awful, but I had no choice but to stay hidden behind the chimney. I was afraid they would hear my footsteps on the roof. The worst part is I had to listen to those evil men boast about what they had done to my family."

"I'm so sorry," Doug said. "How did you finally get away from them?"

"Late in the night things finally quieted down inside the house, so I climbed off the roof and ran from the neighborhood," Phyllis said. "The darkness was frightening, but no worse than the men who were now living in my house. I just kept moving from bush to bush, trying to stay hidden. When sunrise came, I realized I was downtown. The air was thick with the smell of death, and I was horrified at what I saw. There were piles of dead bodies all throughout the downtown parks. I hid myself under an abandoned car and watched in terror as people killed each other for no reason at all. Mothers killing their children—it was horrible."

"You've certainly been through a lot," Doug said. "You don't need to tell me anything else."

Phyllis shook her head. "No, for some reason I feel I need to share it with you. Anyway, I stayed under that car all day, but that night I headed south. I felt I needed to get to Washington D.C., although I had no hope things would be better here. Within a couple of days I reached the 495 Beltway that circles the city. I hadn't seen anyone for a day or so, and in despair I just started walking along the freeway in broad daylight, hoping to see any sign of life. I was almost convinced I was the last person in the entire city. Then I saw the spires of the temple, and I had a strong feeling to come here. The guard at the gate asked me a few questions and then welcomed me inside. It was such a relief to see humans who acted peacefully. They accepted me into the group and taught me the gospel."

Doug smiled at her. "It sounds like the Lord has been watching over you."

She looked Doug in the eye and asked, "So you're telling the truth about a glorious new city where Kansas City used to be? It's a little hard to comprehend."

Doug laughed. "I promise! I'm sure you'll find a wonderful new life awaiting you there."

After breakfast, Billy asked Doug to meet with him and a few other men in the temple visitors center. They discussed several items relating to the group's departure, and they agreed to begin their journey in a couple of days.

As they were wrapping up the meeting, the two friends found themselves alone in the room. Doug noticed Billy had a thoughtful look in his eyes.

"Anything else on your mind?" Doug asked him.

Billy nodded. "Can I ask your opinion about something I've been pondering for the past few weeks?"

"Sure," Doug said.

"Well, from the reports we received, the Coalition forces damaged many buildings in downtown Washington, but they spared the most important buildings, since they felt they would soon be occupying the city themselves. According to our spies, one of the buildings they spared was the National Archives Building."

Billy paused to see his friend's response, but Doug wasn't quite sure what he was referring to. Finally Doug shrugged. "Why would that concern us?"

"You saw the movie *National Treasure* with Nicolas Cage, didn't you?" Billy asked.

"The one where they find hidden messages on the back of the Declaration of Independence? Yeah, I saw it. It was a fun movie, but it was obviously fiction."

Billy smiled. "Yes, the movie plot was fiction, but the building in the movie is really where the nation's most important documents were kept—and apparently in everyone's rush to leave the city during the Coalition invasion, they were forgotten."

Doug started to see what Billy was hinting at. "Are you saying we should see if they're still there?"

Billy was grinning widely now. "I know they would mainly be symbolic in Zion, since the Saints are continuing to follow constitutional principles. From what you've told us, I believe the Elders of Israel's victory over the Coalition fulfilled Joseph Smith's prophecy of saving the Constitution when it was literally hanging by a thread. But wouldn't it be amazing to literally take the original copies of the Declaration of Independence and the U.S. Constitution with us to New Jerusalem?"

Doug felt a wave of excitement pass through him. He was a history buff himself, and it was an intriguing idea. "Yes, I think that would be wonderful. It would be a tangible reminder for the Saints that the Founding Fathers established religious freedom on this land so that the gospel could be restored."

"I feel the same way," Billy said. "I'll organize a group of men to help us, and we'll go into the city first thing in the morning."

✤ ✤ ✤

By early the next afternoon the two friends and twelve other men found themselves on Pennsylvania Avenue standing at a side entrance of the National Archives Building. Doug glanced down the street and looked at the U.S. Capitol and other historical buildings. It was a bizarre sensation to see these American landmarks abandoned with their lawns and shrubbery growing unattended. He felt a sadness creep into his heart to see these poignant reminders of the country he loved.

It had only been a few years earlier that he'd watched President Barack Obama's inauguration on TV. There had been such a feeling of national pride that day. He had been particularly touched to watch former U.S. presidents Jimmy Carter, George Bush, Bill Clinton and George W. Bush all mingle together, while the millions of citizens crowding the Washington Mall rejoiced over the new president's call for responsibility and change. If only things had turned out for the country as everyone had hoped.

"It's so quiet," Doug said to no one in particular. The other men only nodded, appearing to also be dealing with their own emotions.

The group had brought along six handcarts to transport the documents. They figured the documents would still be encased in bulletproof-glass panels, and the handcarts would be used to transport them. The panels would add to their burden as they made their way to New Jerusalem, but they would protect the documents from deterioration.

The men entered the building and made their way to the Rotunda for the Charters of Freedom, which was shrouded in darkness. Doug shined his flashlight on the two large murals on the wall that showed the Founding Fathers signing these precious documents. Then he turned his light toward a series of displays throughout the room.

Just as Billy had suspected, the documents had been abandoned, resting in their protective cases. Although it was going to take a bit of work with a sledgehammer and a crowbar to get them loose, the men would be able to retrieve the documents.

"Hey, at least we don't have to worry about any security alarms going off," Billy said.

A half hour later they had loaded onto the handcarts the Declaration of Independence, all of the pages of the Constitution, and the Bill of Rights.

"Thank you for thinking of doing this," Doug told Billy as they pushed a handcart out of the building. "I know they're just pieces of parchment, but without them, the United States might never have developed into the great country it was. The Saints will certainly appreciate them."

The following morning, Billy and Doug were the last ones to leave the temple grounds, locking the gate behind them. Since no one else had been seen in the area for several months, they didn't feel it was necessary to leave a group of guards behind.

"We'll leave the temple in the Lord's care until a group of Saints can return here someday," Doug said.

The 400 Saints took one last look at their beloved temple and then began working their way west along the freeway system, eager to have a fresh start in Zion.

# CHAPTER 5

⁂

One of the more intriguing places to work in New Jerusalem was a huge metal recycling plant on the western outskirts of what used to be Kansas City. The plant had been refurbished by the Saints and had become a major hub of activity as hundreds of priesthood holders worked to restore—or destroy—the material possessions left behind by American society.

From all across the region, automobiles were being collected for recycling. Since New Jerusalem was functioning on solar power and gasoline was no longer being produced, the cars were being towed to the plant the old-fashioned way. One man would drive a small horse-drawn buggy with the car hooked behind it, while another man sat behind the wheel of the car. It was a slow process, but as hundreds of so-called "car teams" worked together and canvassed the region, thousands of cars had been recycled into usable materials the past several months.

Jonas Ferguson served at the recycling center, and he loved his work. Each day he would receive another car to strip down. Much like the Native Americans had once found a way to use every part of a slain animal, each part of a car was being reused again in some way. The metal was being melted down to create materials for constructing New Jerusalem's newest buildings, and there were many uses for the plastic and rubber. Even music CDs could be melted down, and Jonas got a kick out of seeing the wide variety of music America's former inhabitants had listened to.

"Sheesh, this is quite a collection," Jonas said to himself as he reached into the glove compartment of a minivan and retrieved four CDs: *Def Leppard's Greatest Hits, The Best of Motley Crue*, the soundtrack to *High School Musical 3,* and the debut CD by David Archuleta, the Mormon teenager who became an *American Idol* sensation. Jonas immediately tossed the first two CDs into a recycling canister, but he held onto the last two so he could double-check with his supervisor whether they qualified as "Zion-worthy."

He laughed to himself, remembering when he was employed as a part-time security guard at the E Center in West Valley, Utah. He was working backstage at the David Archuleta homecoming concert way back in the spring of 2009, and he could still hear the screams from the thousands of teenage girls in the audience who cheered his every move.

This job was during Jonas' anti-Mormon days, long before he was baptized into the Church, and he had actually been quite antagonistic about having to work the concert. The kid seemed too squeaky clean and Jonas felt there was no way David could be "the real deal." But Jonas' attitude started to change when David nodded to him before he went on stage and apologized for "causing such a scene."

Then during the concert—as David's upbeat wholesome songs put the crowd into a frenzy—Jonas thought to himself, "Can Mormons really be that terrible if they're able to produce a kid like this?" Jonas went home that night and downloaded David's CD from iTunes, although he never admitted it to any of his macho buddies.

Jonas finished cleaning out the van's glove compartment, then checked his watch. It was Friday, and he was looking forward to the weekend. His friend Tad North had invited him to join his family for Sunday dinner. It was sometimes hard for Jonas to believe the two of them had become such close friends. Tad had never revealed to his family that Jonas had been the CCA officer who had tried to kill him, and Jonas was forever grateful for that. It had allowed him to begin a new life after being baptized and move forward without being labeled for his past deeds.

✦ ✦ ✦

Two days later at the North family's dinner table, Jonas couldn't help but comment about how the North children were growing right up. David was now almost nineteen and taller than his father, while Charles was sprouting right up as a 15-year-old and was quite muscular for a teenager. Meanwhile, 12-year-old Leah was a happy, beautiful girl who brightened a room with her laughter.

Jonas was buttering a roll when he asked Tad, "Have you heard anything about the Church's plans for Salt Lake? It's been almost two years since the Saints left there."

"Actually, I have heard some news," Tad said. "Apparently Sherem Campbell is now extremely paranoid about an attack on Salt Lake from the Mormons. According to the missionary spies living in Temple Square, Sherem still hasn't figured out where the Manti group went. He's afraid they'll make a surprise attack any day, so he has posted guards at all of the valley entrances."

"How are his people even surviving without anyone to steal food from?" David asked.

"It sounds like Sherem recruited all the vagabonds in the area to actually start growing gardens this past spring," Tad said. "The missionaries estimate he has about 5,000 followers living within a mile or so of the Capitol Building. Nearly all of them are men, but there are also a few women that live with Sherem."

David frowned. "We could handle 5,000 people! Let's go wipe them out."

Tad smiled inwardly at his son's eagerness, but he said, "The Church leaders are very interested in having the Saints live again in the cities along the Wasatch Front, but Sherem is clearly looking for a fight, and we've all seen enough bloodshed in the past year."

"That's for sure," Emma said. "I don't want to have to worry about you going off to battle again. Besides, you're enjoying your classes at the university, aren't you?"

David nodded. He had to admit that being part of the freshman class at BYU-Zion was definitely exhilarating. The instructors were amazing—and so were the girls, although he was too shy to say much of anything to them.

Their conversation was interrupted as they looked out the window and saw their neighbors starting to pour out into the street. Emma looked at Tad and asked, "What's going on?"

"I don't know."

They all stood up from the table and went outside onto the front porch. A neighbor called out, "Haven't you heard? The prophet just passed away."

# CHAPTER 6

The 14 living apostles were gathered in the prophet's modest home, and Josh Brown spoke quietly with the other apostles in the living room. The prophet had passed away just an hour before, but earlier in the day—despite being in great pain—he had asked each apostle to take a turn kneeling at his bedside so he could pronounce a final blessing on each of their heads.

It reminded Josh of the Old Testament prophet Jacob giving a final blessing to each of his twelve sons before departing this life, and he could hardly think about the sacred experience without getting a lump in his throat. The prophet had made some promises and prophecies in Josh's blessing that were almost overwhelming to contemplate.

Following the blessings, the prophet's energy was spent, and he gave the group a tired smile. He was looking forward to reuniting with his beloved wife who had passed away a few years earlier. Then he lay back on his bed, closed his eyes, and after a few labored breaths, he simply stopped breathing. The great prophet had returned to his heavenly home to join his family and fellow prophets in Paradise.

The next few days were a very emotional time for the entire Church. The prophet's body lay in state inside a newly constructed stake center near the temple site, and thousands of people filed past the casket to say farewell to the leader who had guided them so faithfully for many years. There wasn't a break in the line from dawn to dusk for five straight days until the scheduled time of his funeral.

This outpouring of appreciation and love for the prophet was the result of his unwavering optimism through some very dark times. No one would ever forget his tremendous leadership in inviting the Saints to the tent cities, even though many less-faithful members openly mocked him for it. Then he kept the Saints' spirits up during the turmoil of the Coalition invasion and the collapse of the United States, before personally leading them from the Rocky Mountains to Zion.

Since there wasn't a building large enough to hold all of the Saints who wanted to attend the funeral, the apostles decided to hold the funeral in that same stake center and reserve attendance to the apostles and the prophet's family members, but to broadcast the funeral to stake centers in the cities of Zion across the world. Millions of Saints had watched the broadcast of the funeral and the procession to the small cemetery near the temple site. As the day concluded, the Saints realized a key link to their past was now gone, but they knew greater things still awaited them.

The day after the prophet's funeral, the 14 remaining apostles assembled together in one of the smaller community temples that had recently been dedicated. The senior apostle conducted the meeting, and it was proposed that this revered man be ordained as the next president of the Church. Josh's heart burned within him as the Holy Ghost confirmed to him that this man was the Savior's chosen prophet at that time.

A chair was placed in the center of the room, and the new prophet took a seat as the other 13 apostles gathered around him and placed their hands on his head. The new president of the Quorum of the Twelve acted as the mouthpiece, and the new prophet was set apart as the President of the Church of Jesus Christ of Latter-day Saints and then given a blessing of strength and fortitude as he served as the Lord's representative on earth. Tears were openly shed as the apostles realized this man could very well be the prophet at the time of the Second Coming.

After warmly shaking each of their hands, the prophet invited them to be seated around the table according to their seniority in the quorum. Josh was still the junior member of the quorum, but he knew another apostle would soon be called to fill the vacancy that had been created.

The prophet then extended his hand toward one of the senior members of the Twelve and presented him as his first counselor, while a junior member of the quorum was selected as the second counselor. It would be a powerful, dynamic First Presidency.

Josh was a little surprised that neither of the previous prophet's counselors were retained in the First Presidency, but those brethren didn't appear at all bothered by the change. They seemed content to return to their places within the Quorum of the Twelve and the new duties they would be assigned. Josh caught the eye of one of them, and they gave each other a little smile. Josh admitted to himself he was relieved he wasn't selected as a counselor.

The prophet then moved to the front of the room and said, "Brethren, in the past few days since the death of our beloved leader, the Lord has strongly impressed upon me that the time has come to implement a new form of government. In the past, we have obeyed the laws of whatever government ruled the land, and the church has still prospered. But now is the time to lay the foundation for the Kingdom of God, which will be the form of government throughout the Millennium."

As the prophet looked around the room, he sensed every apostle was in agreement with what he was saying. During the first year in Zion, the Saints had lived peacefully, but any governing had been done mainly under the Church organization of wards and stakes. Now it was time for an actual government to be organized to deal with long-term planning and larger community issues.

The prophet continued, "Joseph Smith laid out the principles of this government, and actually implemented it in Nauvoo during the last year of his life. It is designed to include and represent all people, whether they are Latter-day Saints or not. We as the apostles will still be at the head of the ecclesiastical portion of this kingdom, but we won't be serving as the governing officers of the kingdom. The main governing body will be composed of men and women known as the Council of Fifty. We will establish it here first in New Jerusalem, and then it will soon be implemented in cities of Zion across the land."

The apostles nodded their heads. They had each heard about the Council of Fifty, and they knew this legislative body was similar in design and purpose to the U.S. Congress. The formation of this council was another step toward having everything ready for the Savior's Second Coming and millennial reign, when he would take his rightful place at the head of the kingdom.

The prophet also explained that the Kingdom of God would be based on the main principles established by the Founding Fathers of the United States, including the U.S. Constitution, and the new government's primary purpose would be to promote order and unity. The prophet then took a book from a nearby table and opened it up. He then asked, "What should be the symbol of this new government?"

The other apostles were quiet, figuring he was going to give them the answer anyway. He chuckled a little, then said, "I'm holding a volume of the *Journal of Discourses.* Let me read you what Brigham Young told the Church in 1855. He said, '*When the day comes that the Kingdom of God will bear rule, the flag of the United States will proudly flutter unsullied on the flag staff of liberty and equal rights, without a spot to sully its fair surface; the glorious flag our fathers have bequeathed to us will then be unfurled to the breeze by those who have power to hoist it aloft and defend its sanctity.*'"

The prophet looked up from the book and said, "It has been approximately 160 years since President Young made that statement, and in that time thousands of our fellow Saints have fought and died for the liberty that flag represents. I can't think of a better symbol of our devotion to freedom."

The other apostles voiced their support, and one of them said,

"President Ezra Taft Benson had felt that the U.S. flag would always fly over this nation, and I feel it's the right thing to do. We no longer have fifty states, but the stars on the flag can represent the Council of Fifty and the rights that the flag has always stood for."

"Very good," the prophet said. "I like that."

He then assigned three of the senior apostles to work together on how to best implement the Council of Fifty and to report at their next meeting on how to introduce the new form of government in a clear manner to the full membership of the Church.

As the meeting came to a close, the prophet said, "As you know, this afternoon at 3 p.m. we'll all be in attendance at a press conference at the Church Administration Building, and I want to share an impression I have received. I feel as we seek to establish a Zion society that is holy and righteous, we as a people need to wear clothing that matches that goal."

He looked around the room at his fellow brethren in their dark suits and colored ties. "I don't know about you, but after everything we've been through, these dark suits remind me too much of the greed and scandal of the previous corporate world. I propose that from this point forward, beginning today at the press conference, that we be clothed in our white suits as we perform all of our official functions. The Saints have seen us wearing those suits at temple dedications, so it isn't completely out of the ordinary. I just feel that we should set the example. Any comments on this?"

Josh raised his hand. "I think it's a good idea. As the Saints have settled into Zion, I've noticed worldly fashion trends beginning to creep back in among us, and it makes me uncomfortable. I don't think we can ask for everyone to suddenly start wearing white all the time, but I don't think it would hurt to ask the Relief Society and Young Women presidencies to start gently emphasizing light-colored clothing while moving away from overly bright or darker colors."

The prophet smiled. "Those are my thoughts exactly. I also

think this emphasis will help the Saints maintain the high level of modesty that we have established here in Zion. I know this change in style won't happen overnight, but each day we move closer to becoming a celestial city, and when the Savior comes again, I envision this people clothed appropriately."

A couple of hours later the prophet introduced the new First Presidency to the world, and there was overwhelming enthusiasm from the Saints about their new leaders. The other apostles were seated at the side of the room, all dressed in white suits. As the press conference ended and the apostles began to mingle with those in attendance, Josh nudged his good friend Elder Smith with his elbow and said, "Hey, you clean up real nice."

Elder Smith chuckled. "I think I'll get used to this new dress style really fast. Most of my dark socks are getting holes in them anyway."

Josh returned home that evening, and immediately the twins crawled toward him. He played with them for a minute, then he gave Kim a hug. She gave him a smile and said, "I'm very happy with the prophet's choice in counselors—and I'm glad you weren't one of them."

"I am, too. But being the youngest apostle pretty much assured I wouldn't be. I'm happy with my current assignments."

Kim looked him up and down. "All of the apostles looked nice in their white suits, but I can't remember you actually wearing it home. Is this a new trend?"

Josh gave her a grin. "You know how I always fret about what color of tie to wear? That shouldn't be a problem anymore."

He explained the prophet's suggestions about lighter-colored clothes, and Kim readily accepted the idea. But Josh soon caught Kim laughing to herself. "What's so funny?" he asked.

"I just never thought you'd become a fashion trendsetter."

Josh shook his head. "Believe me, neither did I!"

# CHAPTER 7

Mark and Michelle Dalton had been serving at the Provo Temple as missionary guards for nearly a year. They knew their service was valuable in helping maintain and protect the temple, but at times they wished they could be in New Jerusalem with their daughter Emma and her family, and also with their son Doug's family. They and the other missionary couples they were serving with had gathered around the temple's computer to watch the satellite broadcast of the press conference announcing the new First Presidency. They knew the new prophet would carry the Church forward in amazing ways.

However, Mark knew there was another reason he and Michelle were still in Provo—and he couldn't even tell her about it. Mark had waited more than ten years for this new prophet to take his place at the head of the Church, and now he could begin one of his final missions in life.

It certainly wasn't a mission Mark had sought after. It had really come about because of a teenage hobby. When Mark was growing up in Springville as a young man in the early 1970s, his uncle Gary had caught "gold fever." At that time, a few books and newspaper articles had been published about the legendary sacred Native American gold mines in the Uinta Mountains in northeastern Utah, and Mark had spent many days with Gary hiking through the mountains looking for them.

Mark and Gary had found many abandoned mines during their searches, and they had even trespassed onto the Ute Indian reservation once to follow a promising lead, but they didn't find any gold. Mark had felt very nervous the entire time they were on the reservation, because it was well-known among goldseekers that the Utes kept a close watch on the sacred mines. Anyone who tried to sneak onto the reservation in search of gold usually found himself with a shotgun in his back as a Ute guard escorted him off the land with orders to never return—or else.

The subject of sacred gold had been a part of Mormon history almost from the moment the Saints set foot in the Salt Lake Valley in 1847. Most of the stories were tied to Thomas Rhoades, an early convert to Mormonism. Thomas led the first expedition of Mormon settlers to northern California in 1846, ending up near Sutter's Fort. Gold was soon discovered there, which triggered the California Goldrush. Much of Thomas' early fortune came from mining the gold-rich fields of the Sacramento Valley.

After the Saints began settling the Salt Lake Valley, President Brigham Young asked Thomas to come to Salt Lake to help finance the Saints' new community. Thomas soon journeyed to Salt Lake with $17,000 in gold.

After Thomas' arrival, Brigham Young had a mint built so a currency of gold coins could be created. Thomas deposited approximately $10,000 of his own gold into the mint account, from which a majority of the territory's gold coins were struck.

In the early 1850s, President Young struck up a friendship with the powerful and influential Ute Indian Chief Wakara. This friendship brought about a general peace between the Indians and the Mormons, and Chief Wakara and many members of his tribe were baptized into the Church.

Soon afterward, Chief Wakara told President Young about a sacred gold mine in the nearby mountains. The chief told the prophet the gold was only to be used for Church purposes, and that only one "white man" could ever know the mine's location. As President Young pondered who that man should be, Thomas Rhoades seemed the obvious choice. At the time, he was serving as Salt Lake City's treasurer, plus he had proven himself to be an honest man in his earlier dealings with the California gold.

After making a pact of secrecy, Chief Wakara took Thomas to the sacred mine. During the next few years, he made several trips into the Uinta Mountains, returning with loads of gold that the Church mint used to create coins such as the ones known as "Brigham's Bees."

During the summer of 1855, Thomas became very ill, and Chief Wakara allowed Thomas' son Caleb to take over the duty of hauling gold from the mine. That same year, Chief Wakara passed away and his successor, Chief Arapeen, renewed the gold pact with Caleb. But Caleb died in 1869, and after the death of Chief Arapeen, the new Ute leader, Chief Tabby, refused to renew the gold pact with the Church. From that day forth, the location of the mine had remained a mystery to outsiders.

Based on this historical evidence and the amount of gold the Church minted in the mid-1800s, researchers believed that a mine really did exist somewhere on the Ute reservation. They pinpointed the location as being somewhere in the Uinta Mountains not far from King's Peak, Utah's tallest mountain. In fact, over the years a few goldseekers had claimed to have found the mine and seen gold artifacts, but when they tried to return, they hadn't been able to locate it again.

However, one "white man" knew the location—Mark Dalton. In 2002, a few more books were published that claimed to reveal the location of the sacred mine. The books weren't specific enough to really lead anyone to it, but as Mark read the information he knew exactly where the authors were talking about, because it was the same canyon he and his uncle Gary had explored when they had gone onto the Ute reservation many years before.

Gary had since passed away, but as Mark read these books, he felt compelled to make one final search for the sacred mine. He didn't go in search of riches—he just felt compelled to know the location of the sacred gold. So one Saturday in the summer of 2004 he woke up at 4 a.m. and knew it was the day to seek out the mine. He prayed once more to confirm that this was the right decision, and a peaceful feeling of assurance came over him.

He left Michelle a note that he had gone for a hike, then he made the drive up Provo Canyon to Heber City, before heading south on Highway 40 to Strawberry Reservoir. From there he traveled to the town of Roosevelt, where he refilled his truck just as the sun was rising. Next he headed north on a small paved road into the Uinta Mountains. His heart was pumping hard, because it felt as if the location of the mine was imprinted on his mind, even though he hadn't been in the area for many years.

After driving several miles he had pulled the truck off to the side of the road and began hiking along a small trail. He knew he was now on the Ute reservation, which only increased his heart rate. To get his bearings, he pulled out a map he had copied from one of the books, and as he looked up from the map, a ray of sunshine burst through the trees and illuminated a small knoll halfway up the mountainside, matching the scene he already had pictured in his mind.

Mark scrambled up the hillside and reached the small knoll, then began studying the rocks scattered there. One flat stone looked like it had been there for centuries, but as Mark stood on it, he felt it shift slightly. He climbed to the side and gave the rock a push. To his surprise it pivoted just enough to reveal a small opening into the knoll. He cleared away the dirt from the opening and shined his flashlight inside, which revealed a large cavern.

He licked his lips nervously and looked around him. It didn't appear anyone was following him, so he squeezed through the opening. Once he was inside the cavern and shined the light around, he realized he was actually in a small man-made room. The floor was smooth and level, and the walls had clearly been hewn out of the rock by tools. He also saw that this little room connected to other rooms.

Mark spotted a buffalo hide that was covering something in

the far corner of the room, and he carefully lifted one corner of the hide. He nearly fainted at the sight. There were at least 500 bars stacked three feet high, and for a moment he let images of a wealthy lifestyle fill his head. He picked up one of the gold bars, which was surprisingly heavy. He began to put it in his backpack when suddenly he felt an ancient spirit beside him. The spirit put a hand on Mark's shoulder and said forcefully, "Put the gold back! This is not the time."

Mark dropped the gold in fright, then he quickly picked up the bar and placed it back on the stack. The spirit moved forward and motioned to the buffalo hide, and Mark put it back as he had found it.

Mark's skin was crawling as if he'd been caught doing something awful, but then he remembered the strong prompting he'd had that morning to wake up and find the mine. Certainly there had to be a righteous purpose behind it.

He didn't dare look at the spirit directly, but he said, "I was led to this gold. Do you know why?"

The spirit didn't respond immediately, as if he was evaluating Mark. Finally the spirit asked, "Are you willing to humble yourself and do the Lord's will?"

"Yes," Mark said. "I got greedy for a moment, but I've come to my senses."

"That is good," the spirit said. "Look."

It seemed to Mark as if the cavern's surroundings were fading away and soon he was standing outside a magnificent temple with beautiful golden beams forming a towering spire. At the temple doors stood a man that he recognized as a member of the Quorum of the Twelve.

Mark heard the spirit say, "When this man becomes president of the Church in a few years, you must return to this sacred place. At that time a way will be provided for you to take the gold to the celestial city for use in building the temple."

The glorious vision faded away, and it left Mark feeling amazed and humbled. For the first time he looked directly at the visitor and saw a middle-aged spirit with Native American features who seemed to glow from within.

"But who prepared the gold bars?" Mark asked him. "It looks like they've been here for centuries."

"You're right," the spirit said. "This gold was mined here and prepared by the righteous Nephites and Lamanites after the Savior's visit to them. During his visit, he told them about the mighty temple that would be built in the latter days, and they yearned to be a part of it. So he gave them directions to this sacred mountain and the gold it contained, and he promised them that if they mined the gold and prepared it so it could be transported, it would be used to build the temple."

"That makes sense," Mark said. "But why am I involved?"

"You agreed to this assignment in the premortal life, and you've been placed in a position on earth that will make everything work out," the spirit said. "Don't worry, if you had become unworthy for the calling, you would have been removed and another man would have taken your place."

"Well, I suppose that's comforting," Mark said with a shake of his head. "What do I do now?"

"Nothing. The time to retrieve the gold hasn't come," the spirit said. "Simply wait until then. Soon there will be great commotions in the earth, and the Saints will return to Missouri and build New Jerusalem. At that time the Lord will place you in a position to be able to accomplish this task. It will require some patience, but the day is fast approaching."

"Should I go talk to the prophet about this?" Mark asked. "Or my wife?"

"There isn't a need to tell anyone else. The Church leaders will be made aware of the gold at the proper time, and your wife isn't required to carry this burden. Now close the cavern entrance and don't return here until the man you saw in the vision stands at the head of the Church."

The spirit seemed to evaporate, and Mark found himself standing alone again in the cavern. He slumped to the ground, suddenly exhausted. It took him several minutes to recover his strength, and as he lay there, he shined his flashlight further down the cavern into the other rooms. There were many other stacks of gold bars protruding out from under buffalo skins. "Wow, the Nephites sure put a lot of effort into this," he said to himself.

He soon squeezed back through the opening and pushed the rock back in place. He stacked a few other rocks around it to make sure no one else was going to accidentally discover it. Then he quickly walked back to his truck and hadn't returned to the area since.

Now several years later Mark was still in awe at how the Lord's purposes had all fit together. The man Mark had seen in the vision had quietly been serving as an apostle in 2004 and there had been several apostles with more seniority ahead of him. But the others had passed away, and now that same man was looked upon by millions of Saints as the Lord's earthly mouthpiece.

As a final indication that the time had come to retrieve the gold, Mark had recently received an e-mail message from his daughter Emma. She had described the tour of the temple site she had taken with Tad, and for some reason she mentioned that the temple beams were nearly ready to be gold-plated. The message had sent a surge of adrenalin through him, and he knew the Lord would somehow help him transport the gold to the temple site.

Then two days later came the most startling message of all—an e-mail to Mark from the new prophet himself. It was straight to the point, and again confirmed to Mark that everything about the sacred mine was true. It read:

*Brother Dalton, I have been informed that the time has come for you to complete your assignment in the Uinta Mountains. Go immediately to Bottle Hollow Reservoir near Roosevelt, Utah. When you arrive there, ask to meet with Ute Chief Milton Natchees. Follow the Spirit and you'll find success in your efforts.*

A few seconds later another e-mail arrived from the prophet:

*You can tell your sweet wife everything now. She deserves to know. Take her with you, and bring her to Zion to see her grandkids.*

Mark dropped to his knees in gratitude. He knew the only way the prophet could know of his mission—and of his desire for Michelle to know about his assignment—was from a source beyond this world.

Mark immediately found Michelle in another part of the temple and took her to a quiet room where they could be alone. He showed her the prophet's e-mails, then he spent the next thirty minutes explaining to her their upcoming assignment. She was a bit overwhelmed, but enthusiastically said, "Let's do it!"

# CHAPTER 8

The next morning Mark showed the other couples at the Provo Temple the first e-mail from the prophet, and they all wanted to know more about it, but he told them, "I can't share anything else, but it will make sense soon. I promise."

There was a collection of bicycles in the temple basement that the guards rode in the parking lot for exercise, and Mark and Michelle felt that bicycling would be the best way to make their journey. They each chose a suitable bike, loaded their backpacks with food and water, then started down the hill toward University Avenue. There hadn't been much repair work done to the streets of Provo following the devastating earthquake and subsequent flood, but enough travelers had passed through Provo Canyon that there was now a small trail worn down to the pavement of the old highway.

Even so, the Daltons weren't exactly youngsters anymore, and the bike ride up the canyon and then toward Strawberry Reservoir was grueling. Four days after leaving Provo they finally pedaled through Roosevelt, Utah and made their way a couple of miles east on Highway 40 to the small reservoir known as Bottle Hollow, just as the prophet had instructed them to do.

During their journey they hadn't seen anyone else, but as they approached the reservoir they could see dozens of people walking around near the water. It wasn't long before the Daltons were spotted, and a man carrying a rifle hurried toward them. "Stop right there," he shouted, and the Daltons cautiously got off their bikes. Mark raised his hands and said, "We aren't here to cause any trouble. We're here to see Chief Milton Natchees."

The mention of that name seemed to surprise the man. "Are you friends of his?"

"I'm hoping he'll be expecting us."

The man eyed them warily. "This land belongs to the Ute tribe, so I'm curious why you're even here."

"I understand," Mark said, "but I think Chief Natchees will be very happy to hear what we have to say. If not, we'll leave immediately."

The man still looked nervous about even talking to them, but after searching them for weapons, he said, "Follow me. Chief Natchees is inside the main lodge."

The Daltons walked behind the man, pushing their bikes toward a large two-story wooden structure that looked like it once functioned as a store. The man turned to them and said, "Lean your bikes against the building, and I'll go talk to the chief."

He disappeared through the doorway, and the Daltons stood outside on the porch. Several Ute children gathered nearby and shyly waved to them. The Daltons waved back, but their minds were focused on how Chief Natchees would respond to their arrival.

"What if he doesn't want to see us?" Michelle asked.

"He will," Mark said, although at that moment he wasn't too sure himself.

They heard a conversation coming through an upstairs window, and they heard a deep voice say loudly, "Don't keep them waiting! The time has finally come."

Within seconds the same man returned with a smile. "You were right. Chief Natchees is waiting for you."

He led them into a small office where an older man with graying hair stood to greet them. He stepped forward and shook their hands warmly. "I'm Chief Milton Natchees. You must be the Daltons."

Mark and Michelle looked at each other in surprise, since they hadn't shared their names with anyone during their journey. Chief

Natchees laughed at their response. "Yes, I know who you are, and I've been expecting you."

"How is that possible?" Michelle asked. "Did someone from the Provo Temple contact you?"

Chief Natchees shook his head slightly. "I'm guessing you are open to matters of a spiritual nature?"

Mark nodded. "You could say that."

"Then let's just say last night that my great-great-grandfather Chief Wakara woke me up to tell me you were on your way."

The Daltons looked at each other, uncertain how to respond, so the chief continued, "Mark, Chief Wakara also told me about your experience with him in the cavern several years ago. He said he couldn't let you get away with that gold bar."

Mark's mouth hung open momentarily. "That was Chief Wakara?"

"Yep. He's been guarding the gold from intruders ever since his death. He said he made every hair on your body stand on end."

Mark smiled, a little embarrassed. "That was me, all right. So you understand our purpose for coming here?"

"Absolutely," the chief said. "Our people have waited for this day for centuries. We've always known the gold was prepared and preserved for use in the great temple of the last days. When I first learned that New Jerusalem would someday be built, I knew deep inside I would somehow play a role in it. My tribe's traditions and the LDS teachings merged so well, and it's an honor to be a part of it."

Mark felt a surge of emotion rise in his chest and said, "I feel the same way."

Then Mark pulled out of his pocket a folded sheet of paper that contained the prophet's e-mail to him. He handed the message to Chief Natchees, who read it and was touched by it. His eyes were a little misty as he looked up and said, "I'm willing to bet that Chief Wakara paid a visit to the prophet as well."

⚜ ⚜ ⚜

Even before the Coalition invasion, Chief Natchees and the Elders of the Ute Tribe had been preparing for the day when the gold would be retrieved and taken to Zion. As part of their preparations, the Utes had purchased and retrofitted 30 fuel-efficient, heavy-duty trucks for the sole purpose of transporting the gold. They even had two 18-wheel tanker trucks filled with gasoline stored away for the journey.

The chief had already selected and trained nearly 100 men who were faithful Latter-day Saints to help transport the gold, and within an hour of their arrival, the Daltons were sitting next to Chief Natchees in a meeting with these men. The chief made final assignments to them concerning the trucks and loading the gold.

"There's no time to waste," the chief said. "Brother Dalton told me that his son-in-law is working on the temple, and the central beams are nearly ready for the gold plating. Let's get to work!"

Later that afternoon the Daltons joined Chief Natchees as part of the caravan of trucks traveling to the mine. As they drove into the mountains, Michelle asked the chief, "Would it be all right for you to tell us how your ancestors even knew to prepare the gold?"

"I think that would be perfectly all right," the chief said. "Of course, this is my own version of the facts, combining my tribe's history with what I've learned as a member of the Church. It's a fascinating story. I'm guessing you're both well-acquainted with the stories of the Book of Mormon?"

Michelle nodded. "We are."

"Good," the chief said. "It makes the story easier to explain, since the gold was actually mined and put into gold bars during the two centuries following the resurrected Savior's visit to the Americas. Righteousness had spread throughout North and South America during this time of peace and prosperity, and everything, including gold, had been consecrated to the Lord's kingdom."

"That sounds just like the events described in Fourth Nephi," Mark said.

"Exactly," the chief said. "During the Savior's visit, he spoke often of the magnificent city that would someday be built in the

Americas, and I must add that my people's own oral traditions support that. Anyway, those ancient Saints pleaded with the Lord about how they could contribute to the great city, and he responded that they could prepare gold bars that could someday be transported to the holy city by their descendants. He explained to them that New Jerusalem would be built in a time of turmoil and strife, and the Saints wouldn't have access to gold to beautify the city. But he assured them he would prepare a way for their gold to reach Zion. We're now fulfilling that prophecy."

As they approached the canyon, Mark perked up, recognizing certain landmarks. "Hey, this road wasn't here before."

"That's right. We've built it in the past year. It actually follows the original road that had been covered up over the centuries."

Mark pointed at the hillside. "We're here! There's the rock where I entered the cavern!"

Chief Natchees smiled at him. "Yes, that's one of several small openings into the mine. We recently built an easier way, though."

The fleet of trucks traveled another 100 yards around the side of the hill to a wide area where all of the vehicles had plenty of room to park. A large wooden door had been built into the side of the hill.

Mark chuckled. "Yes, that way in looks a bit easier to enter."

"We won't actually drive the trucks into the mine, since we consider it sacred ground," the chief said. "But we thought it would be okay to back up right to the entrance."

"Sounds good to me," Mark said.

After all of the trucks were parked near the mine entrance, Chief Natchees and the Daltons gathered with the other men outside the door. The chief said to the group, "This is a joyful day for our tribe, but also for our righteous ancestors who prepared this gold for the beautification of Zion."

Members of the group voiced their agreement as the chief put his hands together while looking skyward. "I give thanks to our Heavenly Father that we could be a part of this great event. Many of you have stood guard in this canyon over the years to keep away treasure seekers, and I'm glad you can finally see the fulfillment of your efforts."

Two men swung the door open, and several yards inside everyone could see stacks of gold bars.

"If we work steadily, we can get the trucks loaded tonight and begin our journey in the morning," the chief told the men. "Meanwhile, I'm going to give our guests a tour of the mine."

The chief took Michelle gently by the arm and escorted her inside, with Mark walking behind them. A few feet inside the mine entrance the chief picked up an electric lantern and led them down one of the corridors as the men began stacking gold bars into small crates and loading them into the trucks.

The Daltons walked with the chief for several hundred feet into the mountain, and suddenly they entered a large room whose walls were literally covered with pure gold. Michelle let out an astonished gasp as she saw along the walls were a number of gold masks, statues, and other artifacts, such as two gigantic disks representing the sun, each more than six feet tall. Several other artifacts were carved with intriguing symbols. The most common symbol showed a carved cross with ivy vines woven around the design.

Chief Natchees pointed to the symbol and said, "That same image is embedded in each of the gold bars. It was one of our ancestors' symbols for the Savior, and it indicates the item is consecrated to the Lord."

The Daltons also noticed boxes that contained large numbers of precious stones such as emeralds, rubies, and sapphires. "We'll be taking those to Zion as well," Chief Natchees said. "I'm sure there are places in the great temple where they can be used."

The Daltons and the chief returned to the mine entrance and began helping put bars into crates. By 10 p.m. each of the trucks had been loaded with several hundred gold bars and plastic tarps were tucked around the crates to hide the contents. There were still many more stacks of gold bars in the cavern, but they agreed the trucks couldn't handle any additional weight. The chief said they would have to return after their first delivery to Zion and bring the rest of the gold at a later time. Mark looked at the long line of trucks and couldn't even begin to contemplate the value of their cargo.

"Your ancestors sure outdid themselves," Mark said. "We didn't even include any of the artifacts."

"We'll bring them next time," the chief said.

The fleet of trucks drove back to Bottle Hollow for the night, and the following day they would begin their journey to Zion. It would certainly be one of the most valuable loads ever to make its way along the nation's freeways. The Daltons couldn't wait to see their daughter Emma's face when her aging parents pulled into New Jerusalem with the consecrated riches of the ancient Americans.

# CHAPTER 9

Chief Natchees told the Daltons that over the past few months he had sent a team of men to evaluate the roadways, and it was clear that traveling on I-80 through Wyoming and Nebraska would be the most effective way to reach Zion, especially with the trucks heavily loaded with gold. When the Coalition had invaded the United States, I-80 had been buried under several feet of snow and had essentially been untouched during the attack. When the snow melted, the road was in great shape and hadn't suffered the kind of earthquake damage that I-70 had suffered.

"Another reason to take I-80 is that because of the terrible winter the towns along that route have all been abandoned," Chief Natchees said. "So we shouldn't face any resistance. The next inhabited city is Lincoln, Nebraska, and the residents are actually members of the Church who are expanding Zion."

"How long is it going to take us to get there?" Michelle asked.

"Well, if we start at sunrise and drive straight through to Lincoln, we should be there sometime after dark," the chief replied. "I think we'll only have to stop twice to refuel the trucks. At least we shouldn't have to worry about traffic!"

The next morning everything was in good shape, and all of the people living in Bottle Hollow turned out to see their departure. The trucks first headed northeast on Highway 40, passing through Vernal and continuing on into Wyoming. Once they reached I-80, the fleet cruised along at a steady 85 miles per hour. The Daltons once again shared a truck driven by Chief Natchees. They were at the head of the caravan, and at one point as they climbed a slight hill, Mark stuck his head out the window and looked back at the other 29 trucks, followed by the two 18-wheeler fuel trucks. They stretched back about a half a mile, and it was awe-inspiring to realize that each of those trucks was filled with gold intended for use in the New Jerusalem Temple.

Chief Wakara watched as the caravan approached Laramie, Wyoming. He was standing next to Mathoni, one of the Three Nephites. One was a spirit and one was a translated being, but they shared the same purpose—making sure the gold arrived safely in New Jerusalem. So far everything had gone smoothly, but there was one hitch.

Laramie was the home of the former Wyoming Territorial Prison that had housed some of the West's worst criminals in the late 1800s, including the notorious outlaw Butch Cassidy in his younger days. The prison had closed long ago and had been developed into a tourist attraction, openly advertising that it was haunted.

Unfortunately, that was true. Many of the outlaws who had spent time there during mortality had returned after their deaths, making it a popular destination both for tourists and for dark spirits. Rather than going to Spirit Prison where they belonged, the spirits had remained earthbound with the same carnal urges and cravings they'd had as mortals.

As these spirits hung around the prison, a favorite topic was the good old days of robbing trains. Nothing could quite match that thrill of holding stolen money or gold in their hands.

At the moment, the dark spirits were in an excited frenzy. One of their old spirit pals had shown up, saying he'd been wandering through the Uinta Mountains when he saw a large convoy of trucks being loaded with gold bars. He followed the trucks to Bottle Hollow and heard of their plans to travel on I-80.

The spirit told his pals, "I thought we could have a great time tormenting those truck drivers. Maybe we could even cause them to crash, and we'd have the gold for ourselves. It would be the biggest heist we ever pulled off!"

His plan was well-received, and the spirits threw around some ideas of what to do to the caravan.

"Too bad there aren't any mortals still living here," another spirit said. "Then we could possess their bodies and really do it right. What about the truck drivers? Do you think we could possess them?"

The first spirit shook his head. "I doubt it. They all have the Light with them."

The rest of the spirits shuddered at that news. Mortals with the Light were their worst enemies.

The second spirit said, "I think we should still cause them some trouble, and maybe get ourselves some gold bars. Our combined energy could certainly knock one of the trucks off the road and hopefully kill the passengers. The faster they're going, the easier we can bump them."

The dark spirits spent the rest of the day talking about the damage they were going to the caravan. Finally the first spirit zoomed into the prison and shouted, "Come on! Where are you guys? The caravan is getting closer!"

The spirits followed him out of the prison and rushed toward the freeway. The caravan was still a few miles away, and they stood in a line across the roadway, knowing their combined negative energy could certainly shift a truck off the road if the driver wasn't paying attention.

"Get ready!" they shouted to each other. "Here they come!"

⚜ ⚜ ⚜

Less than a hundred yards away from the dark spirits, Mathoni and Chief Wakara watched with concern. They knew these spirits could cause an accident that might seriously injure or kill Chief Natchees and the Daltons, who were in the convoy's lead truck.

Mathoni said to Chief Wakara, "A big dust devil would be fitting, wouldn't it?"

The chief nodded, and Mathoni stretched his arm toward a large sandy mound near the freeway. By using his priesthood power, he commanded the sand particles to form a vortex more than 300 feet in the air and to move to the edge of the freeway alongside the dark spirits.

The dust devil accomplished two things: it made Chief Natchees and the other truck drivers slam on their brakes, and it also distracted the dark spirits from their devious plan. The caravan slowed to a crawl and cautiously passed the vortex that stayed stationary as it spun next to the freeway. It was quite a sight.

The dark spirits regrouped and exerted all of their negative energy to try to flip over the lead truck, but it was too late. The truck was going too slowly now for them to have any effect.

The dark spirits sensed there was something supernatural about the dust devil. They looked around and spotted Chief Wakara and Mathoni, and they immediately rushed over to confront them. They didn't recognize these two radiant beings, but they knew they didn't like them.

"Hey, can't you give us a break once in a while?" their leader asked. "We were just going to have a little fun."

"This isn't a joking matter," Mathoni told them. "In fact, all of you need to go back to the Laramie prison and stay there, or I'll have the Light forces come and take you where you belong."

The dark spirits went silent. Some of them had already been to Spirit Prison and didn't like the structured atmosphere there. They preferred the "freedom" of roaming the earth.

Finally their leader said to his pals, "What you do say, fellas? I'm ready to go back to the prison. How about you?"

They didn't need to asked twice. Like a pack of dogs they zoomed off toward the prison where they resumed boasting about their exploits in the good old days.

Mathoni shook his head and said, "What a sad group of men."

He then motioned toward the dust devil, and it instantly stopped spinning, collapsing into a big pile of sand.

He turned to Chief Wakara and gave him a smile. "Well, I'll be on my way. Thanks for letting me know what was going on. I'm glad we were able to help the caravan avoid a problem."

Soon after sunset the caravan reached the western edge of Lincoln, Nebraska, and they could see a pocket of lights not far from the freeway. Before they had left Roosevelt, it had been agreed that the fleet would stop along an exit ramp in Lincoln while Chief Natchees and the Daltons would drive into the city and make sure the inhabitants were friendly. The Utes had equipped each truck with rifles and ammunition in order to defend their cargo if necessary, but they hoped it wouldn't come to that.

When all of the trucks were parked along the off-ramp and accounted for, Chief Natchees drove away from the fleet and toward the cluster of lights, which included an LDS meetinghouse. He parked outside the church, and he and the Daltons went to one the main doors. They were greeted by a younger couple, and they briefly explained that they were traveling with a group from Utah to New Jerusalem.

"We've been traveling since early this morning and we're worn out," the chief said. "Would it be all right if the members of our group slept here tonight?"

"Absolutely," the man said. "We've got plenty of food stored here."

"Very good," the chief said. "I'll let the others know."

Michelle touched the chief's arm. "If it's all right, Mark and I will stay here and help get things ready."

"That would be fine," he said. "I'll be back soon."

The Daltons followed the couple to the kitchen and helped prepare lunchmeat and condiments so when the caravan members arrived they could make sandwiches for themselves. As they worked, the couple explained there were about 50 LDS families living in Lincoln and that the city was well on its way to becoming a city of Zion.

"The way New Jerusalem is growing, we're already almost a suburb," the woman said.

Mark had noticed a laptop computer in a side office, and he asked the man if he had e-mail access to New Jerusalem.

"We do," the man said. "Who do you want to contact?"

"The prophet."

The man's eyes grew a little larger. "The *prophet*?"

"Yep. He's very interested in our caravan."

Mark felt comfortable in sharing some information with him about the cargo the caravan was transporting, and he told the man about the sacred origin of the gold in the trucks.

"Holy smokes," the man said. "Let me get the e-mail program turned on."

Within a couple of minutes, Mark was typing the following message.

*To the First Presidency:*

*This is Mark Dalton reporting on my assignment among the Ute tribe. The gold that has been consecrated for use in the temple has been retrieved. We've made it here to Lincoln, Nebraska, where we will stay for the night. We estimate we should make it to the temple site sometime around noon tomorrow. It's a magnificent sight to see this caravan of thirty trucks all heavily loaded with gold bars. There are still many more gold bars and artifacts in the sacred mine, and the members of the Ute tribe will bring those on a later trip.*

*On a personal note, my wife Michelle and I would love to see our children's families. Would it be possible for someone to notify Tad and Emma North and Becky Dalton that we'll be arriving there? Michelle is so eager to see them that I'm not sure she'll sleep.*

Mark didn't really expect to receive an answer that night, but soon came this response from the prophet.

*Brother Dalton,*

*That is wonderful news. Our construction crews are nearly ready to finish the columns that will form the temple's central spire, so your timing is perfect. Please have the caravan drive directly to the temple construction site. We have a building ready on the site where the gold can be stored. Please thank the brethren for their efforts, and I hope to see you all tomorrow. I'll have my secretary contact your relatives so they can be there as well.*

Mark found Chief Natchees to show him the message, and the chief was thrilled with the prophet's response. By this time, the members of the caravan had gathered in the cultural hall to eat their sandwiches, so the chief stood on a chair and read the prophet's message to the entire group. They let out a spontaneous cheer. The chief smiled and said, "Tomorrow you will meet the prophet of the Lord!"

The Daltons were in awe at the magnificent city that lay before them as the caravan rolled toward the temple site the next afternoon. Emma had tried to explain to them how Zion was growing, but she hadn't conveyed how clean and glorious everything appeared, especially on this sunny morning. For the past year they had watched the city of Provo decay around them, so as they entered this vibrant and colorful city, they really felt like Dorothy Gale did when she woke up in Munchkinland.

Word had already spread throughout the city of the approaching caravan. People began lining the streets and applauding as they passed by.

"Emma had something to do with this crowd," Mark told his wife. "I had a feeling that once the prophet's secretary contacted her, she would let the whole world know we were coming."

By the time the caravan reached the temple site, thousands of people had converged on the area. Chief Natchees drove through the gates of the construction site, and he could see the prophet and apostles standing ahead of them on a platform. Meanwhile, Michelle spotted a group of people standing off to the side of the platform.

"There they are!" she cried out as she recognized her family members.

The truck had barely stopped before she leaped out and ran

toward them. Emma was the first to reach her, and they embraced as only a mother and daughter can who have been separated for so long. Mark was right behind her, and he gave Doug's wife Becky a hug, then gave Tad an embrace as well before the grandchildren swarmed around them.

Michelle looked around for one special grandchild and found little Daniel standing there. She swooped him up and gave him a big kiss on the cheek. He gave her a wide grin, and soon everyone had tears in their eyes.

Tad couldn't help being a bit of a tease, though. "Look at these two! We walked almost a thousand miles to get here, but they arrive in an air-conditioned Chevy truck!"

Mark laughed. "Tough break, isn't it?"

By now, all of the trucks had parked inside the construction site, and their friend Elder Josh Brown joined the group. "Sorry to interrupt the family reunion," he said, "but the prophet would like Mark and Michelle to join him on the platform."

The crowd had surged through the gate onto the temple main plaza, which was now completed. The prophet introduced the Daltons and spoke briefly about their role in bringing the gold to Zion. Then he introduced Chief Natchees and handed the microphone to him. The chief repeated the story he had told the Daltons of how the gold had been mined by the righteous Nephites and Lamanites, and of the Savior's promise to them that the gold would someday be their contribution to the holy temple.

The chief could barely contain his emotions as he concluded by saying, "Today that marvelous prophecy has been fulfilled. I'm so humbled to be here in this glorious city."

He handed the microphone back to the prophet, who said, "We are going to preserve some of these gold bars and put them on display throughout the city so that each of you can see and touch them. They are beautifully engraved, and it's a shame that we'll have to melt down the rest of them, but that's their purpose."

The day turned into a mini-holiday of rejoicing and celebration as the Saints realized how close the temple was to being completed.

It was also a reminder of what a special city they were living in. Saints from all generations since Adam and Eve had looked forward to the building of New Jerusalem, and now they were a part of it.

# CHAPTER 10

As the celebration was winding down that evening at the temple plaza, Josh Brown felt a tap on his shoulder. He turned around to see his good friend Mathoni, one of the Three Nephites.

Josh grinned and shook his hand. "Hello, stranger. I haven't seen you for a while."

"I've been tied up with a few projects lately," Mathoni said. "Actually, I've been shadowing Mark and Michelle Dalton ever since they left the Provo Temple. I was as eager as anyone to see the gold arrive here safely. Don't forget, I was there when the Savior made that promise to my people."

"Were the Daltons ever in any danger?" Josh asked.

"Just a couple of times. Satan knew what their journey would lead to, so he prompted some men to attack them in Provo Canyon, but I scared them off by rolling a few well-placed boulders down the mountain. The Daltons never even noticed. Then in Wyoming I used a mini-tornado to distract some evil spirits from causing trouble. You know, just doing my usual line of work."

Josh laughed. "I've sure missed you. But having this gold arrive today reminded me we still have a busload of plates waiting in Hopiland that need to be brought here."

"I was thinking the same thing. It might be a good time for us to retrieve them. Let's go talk to the prophet about it."

"I believe he was heading back to his office after the celebration," Josh said. "We should be able to find him there."

The pair went to the Church Administration Building, where

Josh let them inside. As they walked down the hall, they could see the prophet's office door slightly ajar. Josh knocked lightly and said, "President? It's Elder Brown. Do you have a moment?"

They heard someone shuffle some papers, then they heard, "Why, yes. Come right in."

Josh and Mathoni entered the room, and Josh prepared to introduce Mathoni. Instead, the two men walked toward each other and gave a quick embrace. "You're looking as good as usual," the prophet told the Nephite, giving him a wink.

"Never felt better," Mathoni said.

They turned toward Josh, who was surprised by their friendly banter. "I didn't know you two were acquaintances," he said.

Josh wasn't really surprised by this news. It was just he had somehow considered Mathoni to be *his* Nephite.

The prophet smiled. "Yes, we go way back. I think it was at President Benson's funeral in 1994 that we first met, wasn't it?"

"That's right," Mathoni said. "By the way, congratulations on your new calling. You'll do well."

The prophet shrugged. "I've got some big shoes to fill, but with the Lord's help I'll do my best. So, what can I help you two with this evening?"

Josh took a minute to explain to the prophet about the busload of engraved plates he and Mathoni had removed from a cave in Central America, and how the plates were now hidden in a bus in the Arizona desert.

"At the time, the Coalition soldiers were still roaming the land and we hadn't established New Jerusalem yet," Josh said. "But now we can bring them to you so that they can be translated."

"Yes, please bring them here. I'm eager to see them." Then the prophet paused before adding, "Let me show you something."

He went to a desk drawer and pulled out a medium-sized box. He clicked open the box's combination lock and carefully lifted out an item that resembled old fashioned spectacles, with clear triangle-shaped stones for lenses.

"Do you know what these are?" he asked.

"The Urim and Thummim?" Josh responded excitedly.

The prophet nodded. "I haven't been able to use these as often as I would like, and I'd love to start working on the plates. Mathoni, do you have your usual transportation available?"

"I do. We'll return as soon as possible."

The prophet was referring to one of the few material possessions on earth that Mathoni considered his own—a blue Nissan four-door that had been given to him by a General Authority in the late 1990s to use on various Church-related errands. Mathoni had kept the car maintained and stored away—along with plenty of gasoline tanks hidden in various locations between Utah and New Jerusalem.

As a translated being, Mathoni could zip across the country in a split second if he needed to, but the car had come in handy when he needed to help mortals with some of their earthly errands. Right now the car was locked in a garage in Wichita, Kansas.

As the pair walked out of the building, Mathoni told Josh, "If you would like to go tell Kim that you'll be gone for a couple of days, I'll go get the car and pick you up in about two hours."

"Sounds good."

✢ ✢ ✢

Since Mathoni never needed to sleep, he drove the car all night as Josh got some rest. By early morning they arrived at the canyon on the Hopi reservation in Arizona where the bus was hidden. Mathoni parked the car across the dirt road to block easy access into the canyon, then they walked the remaining quarter-mile to the pile of rocks that completely covered the bus.

Mathoni got right to work, using the priesthood to move the rocks from the front and the back of the bus. Josh hadn't noticed before how Mathoni had placed rocks under the bus to keep it off the ground a little and take pressure off the tires. Once those rocks were in a tidy pile off to the side, Mathoni paused a moment to inspect the tires.

"They've held up pretty well, but we'll check their pressure before we drive off," Mathoni said. "I've got an air compressor in the trunk of the car."

Then he turned to Josh. "Okay, it's your turn."

"What do you mean?" Josh asked in surprise.

"It's time for some priesthood training," Mathoni said. "You're an apostle of the Lord, and you have the power to move mountains—so a few rocks shouldn't be too hard."

"Are you saying . . ."

"Yes. You've seen how I do it. Now go ahead and do it the same way."

Josh frowned. "But I don't think I can."

"It's all a matter of faith. Remember how the Savior commanded the storms to cease and the blind man to see? The very elements of the earth will heed the command of a righteous priesthood holder, if it's the Lord's will."

"I understand that, but why can't *you* just move them?" Josh asked. "Aren't we in a hurry to get back to Zion?"

Mathoni became a little impatient. "Do you think this is just a game? There's a real purpose behind this. You're going to need these skills someday soon."

There was a moment of silence, as they both realized that Mathoni had unintentionally given Josh a hint about his future. But rather than asking further questions, Josh took a deep breath and approached the bus. There were still two dozen rocks that needed to be moved before the bus could be driven away.

Josh focused on a three-foot-high boulder near the front of the bus. Through the priesthood, he commanded the rock to rise, and to his amazement, it wobbled upward a few inches.

"Good job," Mathoni said. "Now move it away from the bus."

Under Josh's command, the rock continued to elevate. It clunked twice against the side of the bus, but then it moved away and settled onto the pile of rocks that Mathoni had started earlier.

"Whew, I did it!" Josh said with a mixture of relief and confidence. It had taken a huge amount of concentration, and he wiped away beads of sweat from his brow.

"Excellent," Mathoni said. "It gets easier each time. Just keep going."

Josh pointed at another rock and commanded it to rise. It moved five feet into the air before Josh started chuckling. The rock immediately crashed to the ground.

"What's wrong?" Mathoni asked.

Josh grinned. "I realized that I had my hand outstretched and pointing at the rock like they do in the movies. I suddenly felt like Charlton Heston as Moses in *The Ten Commandments*. Is it really necessary?"

"No, but if it helps you to focus on a particular rock, then go for it."

Over the next ten minutes, Josh successfully moved the remaining rocks away from the bus. It was a bit mind-boggling to him, and he humbly gave all the credit to the Lord and the power of the priesthood. Once the final boulder was out of the way, Mathoni opened the bus door and looked around inside. "We're in good shape. The plates are just as we left them. I've got sixty gallons of fuel hidden in a small cave behind the bus. Let's fill up the tank and be on our way back to Zion."

After filling the fuel tank, they drove the bus to the car, where they added some air to the tires with the compressor. Then Mathoni parked the car a few feet off the road and climbed into the bus.

"Are you going to just leave the car here?" Josh asked.

"Yes. It'll be fine. I'll come back for it soon."

As had been the arrangement when the pair had driven from Guatemala, Mathoni drove the bus to Missouri while Josh sat in the passenger seat. It didn't really need to be said—with so many valuable plates on board, the bus was much better off in the hands of a translated being. Mathoni could be talking animatedly as he described to Josh something he had witnessed—such as the three days of darkness in the Americas after Christ's crucifixion—yet he never crossed the road's center line.

After a full day of nearly non-stop driving—Josh had again slept for several hours along the way—Mathoni pulled the bus into a parking lot behind the Church Administration Building. Josh hurried inside the building and spoke briefly to the prophet's secretary, who ushered him into his office.

"Did you complete your assignment?" the prophet asked.

Josh nodded eagerly, and the prophet smiled. "Let's go see what you've brought."

They met Mathoni in the parking lot and entered the bus. Mathoni had removed the blankets from the dozens of plates, and the sight was quite breathtaking.

Mathoni pointed to a row of plates near the bus door. "I know all of the translating of the plates must be done by mortals, but if I may make a suggestion, I would focus on these sets first. I put these sets here because these are the records Mormon referred to most often when he made his abridgement that became the Book of Mormon. I think the Saints would find those records the most interesting."

Mathoni then turned and picked up a set of plates that was resting in one of the front seats. "However, I would start with this set first."

The prophet looked at the plates curiously. "Are these what I think they are? The brass plates?"

Mathoni nodded. "Yes, the same plates that Nephi killed Laban for and brought from Jerusalem."

"The prophet's eyes lit up. "I'd love to start translating them as soon as possible. Elder Brown, please carry them inside."

⊹ ⊹ ⊹

After the brass plates and the other specified sets of plates had been taken to the prophet's office, Mathoni parked the bus right next to the building's back door and offered to move the rest of the plates to a storage room.

"I can help you," Josh told him.

"Well, you can keep everyone out of the hallway," Mathoni

said. "I can work quickly, but I'd hate to plow anyone over."

"Sounds good," Josh said. For the next several minutes he guarded the hallway as Mathoni repeatedly dashed past him, seemingly just a blur. Soon the Nephite was done with the task, and he didn't even look tired. He led Josh into the storage room and they admired the full shelves of ancient records. Mathoni pointed to the closest shelf and said, "I organized them in chronological order to make the translating easier."

"That's wonderful," Josh said. "I'll let the prophet know."

Mathoni then put his hand on Josh's shoulder. "Thank you for everything you're doing. I'll park the bus in one of my hiding places and retrieve my car, but then I'm off to another assignment."

Josh was disappointed. "I was hoping you'd be sticking around for a while. When will I see you again?"

"Don't worry, we'll be working together again soon."

Later that same day the prophet called a special meeting for all of the apostles. He had brought the brass plates into the room, and they rested on the table in front of him. The apostles were very curious about them, and some wondered if they were the golden plates, but it was clear they were made of a different metal.

The prophet smiled. "I've enjoyed listening to your comments about the item I've brought today for 'Show and Tell.' These are the brass plates that Nephi brought from Jerusalem. We're very blessed to have them and many other plates now in our possession."

The apostles were very excited at the news, and the prophet invited them to come forward to turn the metallic pages and examine the ancient writing.

"How did we receive the plates?" one of the apostles asked.

The prophet motioned toward Josh. "Elder Brown has been extensively involved in this project, even before he was an apostle, and he'll share how this came about. He and Mathoni—one of the Three Nephites some of you have met—have brought us dozens of ancient records, and they're now being stored in this building."

Josh stood and took a few minutes to explain about his service in Guatemala, his interaction with Mathoni, and how the plates had been hidden on the Hopi reservation before being brought to Zion. He concluded by saying, "I've been in the cavern where these plates were stored and can testify of its existence. According to Mathoni, he helped Mormon and Moroni hide these plates there just before the final battle of the Nephites around 385 A.D. They've been tucked away there all these years, and now it's our opportunity to translate them and share them with the world."

As Josh sat down, the prophet thanked him then added, "As Elder Brown mentioned, it's our privilege to translate these records. The plates were written by mortals, and therefore they must be translated by mortals. It would be much easier if we could have Moroni or Mathoni sit down and read them to us, but that's not how the Lord works."

The apostles laughed a little, and the prophet continued, "That means the responsibility for translating these records falls to the 'prophets seers, and revelators' of the Church. In other words, those of us in this room. I'm looking forward to it, and I'm sure the rest of you are as well. However, the ability to translate is a gift of God, and some of us might be better at it than others."

He then removed from his pocket the Urim and Thummim and placed it on the table. The apostles had naturally assumed it was in the prophet's possession, but only a couple of them had actually seen it.

The prophet motioned toward the plates and to the Urim and Thummim. "I'd like each of you to translate a few sentences from the brass plates. I'm sure the rest of us will enjoy listening in as you do so. Let's go in order of seniority."

Josh raised his hand. "President? If I may ask, are you able to translate smoothly?"

The prophet smiled. "Yes, thankfully I've been given that gift, and I read the first few pages of the brass plates earlier today. It's rather fascinating."

Josh waited patiently at the end of the line with Elder Colton

Negus, a native of England, who was called to fill the vacancy in the Quorum of the Twelve soon after the First Presidency was reorganized. Josh had immediately felt a bond with the new apostle, and he particularly enjoyed Elder Negus' dry wit.

"This ought to go well," Elder Negus whispered to him as they waited their turn. "Here's a British lad trying to translate ancient Hebrew to the satisfaction of a bunch of Yankees."

Josh laughed, but inwardly he worried about his own ability. Several of the other apostles were fluent in many languages, and he suspected they would be more adept at translating than he would be. He grew up in California and he'd never learned another language, other than a little Spanish. Then he'd served an English-speaking mission in northern Utah, so he knew the odds were already against him.

He watched the apostle ahead of him confidently sit down and look through the Urim and Thummim at the plates. The apostle immediately began dictating several sentences about the creation of the world. The prophet soon raised his hand to stop him.

"Excellent," the prophet told him, and he stepped out of the way as the prophet motioned for Josh to take a seat.

Josh picked up the Urim and Thummim and peered through them, and it was as if the words on the brass plates were magnified slightly, but they still looked like ancient Hebrew to him.

"Is it supposed to change to English?" he asked.

"Yes," the prophet said. "Just concentrate on a certain set of symbols and empty your mind, letting the Spirit work."

After a few seconds, the words did change to English, but after he said them, he had to refocus on another set of symbols, and it took a few seconds for the words to change. After about two minutes he had read a sentence. He lifted his eyes from the Urim and Thummim and smiled at his fellow apostles. "I might get a whole chapter done by the Second Coming."

The prophet put his hand on Josh's shoulder. "Don't worry about it. You did just fine for your first time."

Elder Negus then took his turn, and did about as well as Josh had. He stood up and said, "President, I'll leave the book work to the older gentlemen, if you don't mind."

The prophet smiled and invited the apostles to return to their seats at the table. Once they were seated, he said, "Thank you so much for making the effort. It's a unique experience, and I think with a little practice each of you would do well. But as Elder Negus mentioned, I do think some of our older brethren seemed more at ease with translating. Besides, we all have many duties to perform beyond translating the plates. So I have selected three brethren who will work with me on our translation team."

He then named three of the senior apostles who had translated extremely well. Josh was satisfied with the selections. Two of these apostles required the use of wheelchairs, and he knew they were a bit discouraged they couldn't get out among the people like they used to. Their new assignment would work out for everyone involved, and Josh marveled at how the Lord continually found opportunities for the apostles to fully serve, no matter their physical limitations. Besides, the words of Mathoni on the Hopi reservation had hinted that another assignment awaited him.

Over the next few weeks, the prophet completed translating the brass plates, and it was published for all the Saints to read. It was a doctrinal and historical goldmine, and everyone rejoiced to read the truths it contained.

Also, the "translation team" spent considerable time working with scribes to translate the more vital and interesting records, such as the Book of Lehi, which was first translated by Joseph Smith but lost when the 116 pages were stolen from Martin Harris. It greatly expanded the Saints' knowledge of Book of Mormon history, and it was exciting to finally know the names of Nephi's sisters, as well as the true relationship between Ishmael and Lehi. These translated works were published in separate volumes by the Church and were known as *The Nephite Plates Series*.

Emma had been privileged to help edit and produce the series of inspiring stories from Saints around the world the previous few months, and now she was part of the staff producing the Nephite series. As part of her work, she was able to bring home some printouts of early editions of the volumes before they actually went to press, and her family members were allowed to read through them and point out any errors they might find. It was fun to see Tad and their children greet her at the door and then run off with the latest copies.

Once the books had been thoroughly edited and double-checked by an apostle, thousands of copies were printed and distributed to each family. During this period the streets of Zion were unusually quiet, since everyone was home reading the latest release in the series. Parents would read some of the more action-based stories to their little children, and soon those stories were as well-known as many of the cherished Book of Mormon stories had been. These new books raised the spirituality of the entire city, and this additional gospel knowledge played a major role in elevating the spirituality of the people.

Emma had heard the prophet was now translating a detailed account of the Savior's visit to the Americas written by Shemnon, one of the Lord's Nephite disciples. The volume was expected to be at least 300 pages long and would include the Savior's complete messages to the ancient Saints.

When Emma told Tad about the upcoming book, he said, "That sounds fantastic!" Then he grinned and joked, "I haven't seen Mormons this excited to read a book since the last volume in the *Twilight* series was released. Bring home a copy as soon as possible."

Emma smiled at his comment, because while she and her husband had actually read LDS author Stephanie Meyers' vampire books in the years before the Coalition invasion, the old "Tadinator" would never have been too eager to read an expanded account of Third Nephi. He had definitely changed!

# CHAPTER 11

Doug Dalton savored the sight ahead of him. He could clearly see the Gateway Arch looming on the horizon, and that meant they were nearing downtown St. Louis. He was sure there would be Saints waiting to greet them. Before he had left on his assignment as one of the 144,000 high priests, he had been part of a planning committee in Denver on how to establish Zion and then expand it. He knew St. Louis would be a major transportation hub for the Saints coming from overseas, with boats bringing the Saints up the Mississippi River to St. Louis before being transported to New Jerusalem on trains.

The past few weeks had been more challenging than he had expected. For the past year, he had been on his own and could travel at whatever pace he wanted. But now he was helping lead approximately 400 Saints from the Washington D.C. temple, and not everyone moved along at the same speed.

The group had chosen to travel to New Jerusalem by walking west on I-70. It was the most direct route, and more importantly, it was the path that the Coalition forces had followed as they made their inland attack. That meant nearly all of the U.S. citizens along that freeway had either been killed or had fled somewhere else, leaving an empty roadway for the Saints.

As expected, they didn't encounter other groups, but it was still depressing to pass through formerly bustling cities such as Columbus, Ohio and Indianapolis, Indiana. The empty crumbling buildings, abandoned vehicles and overgrown parks were a vivid reminder of the difficult times they had lived through. But now those cities were behind them, and better times awaited the members of the group.

Doug had become somewhat of a father figure to Phyllis, the young woman from Baltimore who had joined the group a few weeks before they departed. She soaked up gospel knowledge like a sponge, and their conversations about the history of the Church helped pass the time as they walked along.

Doug sometimes took a turn pushing the handcarts that carried the historical documents he had helped retrieve, and each time he did so created a feeling of patriotism within him. The United States of America no longer existed, but he knew a government founded on these same principles was beginning to emerge in New Jerusalem.

✧ ✧ ✧

The next morning the group approached the eastern side of the Mississippi River across from the Gateway Arch, where they were confronted by a pair of men who were guarding the Martin Luther King Bridge into downtown St. Louis.

"Please stay where you are until you identify yourselves," one of the guards shouted. Doug quickly stepped forward—he was getting used to these confrontations with guards—and slowly started walking toward them with his hands raised.

"My name is Doug Dalton, one of the 144,000 high priests," he called out. "This group has come from the Washington D.C. Temple and want to live in Zion."

His words seemed to satisfy the guards, and they immediately relaxed. "Sorry for the rough welcome," one of them said. "We just have to be cautious. There are still groups out there that pretend to be Saints who then cause us trouble."

The guards helped them across the bridge and gave them directions to Union Station, where they were registered as new members of Zion and were provided a large meal, along with the chance to take a shower and change into new clothes.

Doug explained to the Church officials about the group's long journey across the eastern United States, and he was thrilled when they consented to send an extra train that day so the Washington D.C. group could arrive together in Zion. The train station had a phone link directly to New Jerusalem, and Doug eagerly asked the operator for the number of his wife Becky's home. The phone rang three times, then he heard, "Hello?"

Doug caught his breath then said, "Becky, this is Doug. I'm in St. Louis! I should be there tonight!"

He had to hold the phone away from his ear to avoid going deaf from Becky's happy shriek. "I can't believe it," she said. "Everyone is so eager to see you!"

He gave her the information about when the group would arrive at the main train station in New Jerusalem and said he hoped she could meet them there.

She laughed. "Don't worry, my dear. You can expect a rousing welcome!"

✤ ✤ ✤

Doug hovered nearby as the historical documents were loaded into four large containers that could be wheeled onto the baggage car of the train. The group had made quite a sacrifice to bring them this far, and he wanted to make sure they completed the final stretch. Then he joined the group members as they happily took their seats on the train, basking in a luxury they had sorely missed.

"Now I know how the Saints must've felt in 1869 when the transcontinental railroad was completed. I won't miss our handcarts, that's for sure," Billy Fox told Doug as they settled into the cushioned seats and felt the train start moving.

"Yes, this feels like heaven," Doug answered.

Later that evening the train rolled to a stop in New Jerusalem. Doug looked out the window from his seat and could see Becky and his children standing on the platform, along with Emma, Tad, and their children. Several other relatives had also come to greet him. As Doug departed the train, he was surrounded in the arms of these loved ones, and he couldn't seem to hug them enough. Those lonely nights in Manhattan now seemed like a distant dream. He held his son Daniel, and although Daniel couldn't speak, they shared a tender moment of happiness at being reunited again.

There were also several dozen Saints waiting to greet the new arrivals. The group quickly shrunk as families were taken to the homes that had been prepared for them. Doug was eager to see his family's home—having never been there himself—when he felt a tap on his shoulder. He turned to see Phyllis standing there. She gave him a small wave and said, "Well, I guess this is good-bye for now. I don't have any family here, but Brother Fox said I could stay with one of the families I had gotten to know at the temple."

Doug shook his head, knowing that Phyllis was nervous about being treated as some kind of foster child, even though she was nearly 20 years old.

"Hey, don't go anywhere. We'll find a place for you," he said. "Please come meet my family."

He then introduced Phyllis to his family members and told them a little about her experiences in Baltimore and traveling alone to the Washington D.C. Temple, where she was baptized. She blushed a little and said, "I really don't want to intrude, but Brother Dalton has been such a good friend to me and helped keep my spirits up. I promise I wouldn't be a bother to you."

Emma stepped forward and put her arm around Phyllis' shoulder. "Consider us your family now," she said, and the other family members voiced their agreement.

"Thank you so much," Phyllis said. "After what I've been through, it will be nice to be with people I can trust."

At the back of the group, Emma's oldest son David suddenly felt his heart racing. Phyllis was possibly the most beautiful girl he had ever seen. He'd always been quite shy around girls and hadn't really dated much, and now this girl was going to be hanging around his family? He felt a mixture of joy and fear.

Suddenly his mother turned around and said, "David, come here and meet Phyllis. She's about your age."

"Duh, Mom," David thought as he came forward and shook Phyllis' hand with his very sweaty palm.

"Uh, nice to meet you," he said, and Phyllis smiled at him, intrigued by this clean-cut young man.

Emma turned back to Phyllis. "David is part of the freshman class at BYU-Zion, the new university here. Did you have a chance to attend college before the invasion?"

"Yes, I was going to a junior college at the time."

"Very good," Emma said. "I'm sure you could get enrolled here, and David would be happy to show you around the campus."

David nodded, a little distracted. "That's fine with me."

Tad and Emma glanced at each other, and he gave her a quick wink. Maybe Phyllis could help David break out of his shell.

It was decided that Phyllis could live in a spare bedroom with Michelle Dalton, who had recently moved into a house on the same block as the Norths. Her husband Mark had recently departed with Chief Natchees back to Utah to bring the remaining load of gold bars and artifacts from the sacred mine, and he wouldn't be back for a week or so.

"I'd love to have you stay with me," Michelle told Phyllis. "I'll welcome the company!"

That night David took his patriarchal blessing out of his scriptures and read through it. He had received the blessing when he was 14 years old, a couple of years before the Coalition invasion. It mentioned specifically that he would gain a college education and serve a mission. He could remember reading it while in the tent city in Hobble Creek Canyon and seriously doubted whether any of those events could actually come to pass.

But now he was attending college, and he reasoned that his service with the Elders of Israel could count as a mission—although the blessing spoke of him baptizing hundreds of people, and he certainly hadn't baptized any Coalition members. It still didn't seem realistic, because the Church was currently leaving the missionary work to high priests like his uncle Doug, but anything was possible. David also sensed Phyllis might fit into his life somehow as well, but he knew that he needed to take life one step at a time.

A couple of days later Phyllis stopped by the Norths' home to talk to David.

"I'm sorry to bother you, but I'm hoping you have time to help me get registered for classes," she told him. "I don't have any idea how to get started."

"Sure," David said. "Let's check what classes are available on the computer. Do you have your Zion ID number?"

Phyllis frowned. "Is that the number they gave me during the registration in St. Louis?"

"Yep. It's just a combination of your birthdate and the day you were registered as a member of Zion."

"I left the number at your grandma's house, but we should be able to figure it out."

They went into the house and Phyllis greeted Emma with a quick hug. Then the pair sat down at the computer in the family room and logged onto ZOOM, the Zion Official Online Membership website that contained a database of everyone who had registered as a citizen of New Jerusalem. The Saints used the site to check on whether family members or friends had made it to New Jerusalem, and messages could be sent to each other, similar to the old Facebook website that had been so popular in the previous society.

Phyllis told David her birthdate and arrival date, and he typed in the numbers. Within seconds a screen popped up that showed Phyllis' basic information, along with a photo of her taken when she registered in St. Louis. In the photo Phyllis was glancing sideways and her mouth was partially open as if she were drooling.

"Yep, you're in the system," David said.

"Ooooh, I look horrible," Phyllis cried. "I didn't know they were taking the photo."

"Obviously," David said with a laugh, and she punched him playfully on the shoulder.

"We can get that fixed, can't we?"

"Nope, you're stuck with that one."

Phyllis let out a little scream, and David smiled. "Just kidding. We can take another one of you today and send it to the site."

Phyllis was visibly relieved. They then went to the BYU-Zion registration site and looked at potential classes. "I guess I'll have to start over as a freshman, right? The last I heard, my college had sunk into the Atlantic Ocean."

"I'm afraid so," David said. "The only students that are considered upperclassmen are the people who had been attending either BYU-Hawaii, BYU-Idaho, or BYU-Provo. The Church was able to recover the online data from those schools, even though they aren't operating at the moment."

"That's fine with me," Phyllis said. "Besides, I was hoping I could get some classes with you. I know I'm going to have to study hard to catch up, but maybe we could study together."

"Uh, I think that could work," David said, suddenly feeling like he had just hit a game-winning home run.

They filled out her schedule, and they ended up having three classes together. Phyllis would be able to start attending school the following Monday. She thanked him profusely and actually started crying, saying she was finally feeling happy for the first time since the Coalition invasion.

# CHAPTER 12

Doug Dalton spent his first few days in New Jerusalem getting reconnected with his wife and children, and he had made sure the containers holding the historical documents had been delivered to his home, rather than get misplaced while Billy Fox and the other Washington D.C. members settled into their new homes in the southern part of the city. Finally Doug contacted Billy and asked, "Are we ready to deliver the historical documents to the Church leaders?"

"Yes, let's do it tomorrow if possible."

That night Doug traveled across the city to the Brown home, and Kim opened the door. "Doug! I had heard you were back," she said. "You look great."

"Thanks, but it's easy to keep the weight off when you walk halfway across the United States," he said with a shrug. "I just wanted to see if Josh is home. We brought with us some interesting documents from Washington D.C., and we wanted to present them to the Church leadership."

"Sorry, but Josh is organizing two new stakes on the outskirts of the city, and I don't expect him back until late."

"Organizing stakes on a weeknight?" Doug asked. "I thought that was a Sunday job."

"Not anymore," Kim said. "Zion is growing so rapidly they can hardly stay ahead of it."

"That makes sense," he said. "Anyway, it's wonderful to see you."

"I feel the same way," Kim said. "Hey, now that you're back in town, I'd love to get together with you and Becky and the Norths, just like old times. I think Josh would like a night off to catch up on things as well."

Doug nodded. "That sounds great. I'll let Emma know, and I'm sure she'll be in touch with you."

Doug told Kim that he'd still go ahead and take the documents to the Church Administration Building in the morning, and she said she would let Josh know. "I think tomorrow is their weekly meeting anyway, so that would be good timing," she said.

Early the next morning Billy arrived at Doug's home, and they loaded the document containers into a solar-powered moving van Billy had received permission to use. They drove to the Church Administration Building, hoping to arrive before the apostles began their meeting. Doug went to the front desk, where he told the secretary, "I'm Doug Dalton, a close friend of Elder Brown, and his wife Kim said it would be all right to contact him here today."

The secretary looked a little skeptical, but she paged Josh's office. When he answered, she said, "There's a Doug Dalton here to see you. Do you want to meet with him?"

"Absolutely," came Josh's reply. "I'll be right down!"

Doug tried not to look too smug as the secretary hung up the phone. Within thirty seconds Josh came down the hall and gave Doug a quick embrace. "It's so good to see you again," he said. "Kim told me you had stopped by, and she said something about documents."

Doug nodded and looked over at Billy. "Yes, we've brought some documents the Church should be interested in. In a van outside we've got a few items, such as the original Declaration of Independence and the U.S. Constitution."

Josh's eyes bulged slightly. "Really? That's incredible!"

He recruited some help from other office workers, and soon the containers had been taken from the van to a meeting room, where the glass panels containing the documents had been placed along the walls. The First Presidency had been summoned, and after a brief introduction, Billy and Doug shared the story of how they had rescued the documents from the National Archives Building before they departed from Washington D.C.

Soon all of the apostles had joined them in the room, and there was a sense of reverence as they slowly worked their way along the walls looking at the documents. The Declaration of Independence seemed to gain the most attention.

The prophet took Billy and Doug aside. "I'm sure the Founding Fathers are pleased with your efforts to preserve these items," he said. "I've been thinking that we need to create an American History Museum here in Zion. The United States of America no longer exists, but we certainly need to preserve and memorialize the sacrifices of our ancestors. The children of Zion need to have a sense of history, and these documents will be one of the cornerstones of that museum. Thank you for bringing them here."

A couple of weeks later Kim, Emma and Becky had coordinated their schedules so the three couples could get away for an evening. They had chosen to meet at a place in downtown New Jerusalem that would bring back some memories for all of them. Someone had built a pizza parlor that was a replica of Provo's Brick Oven Restaurant. In some ways it was a little corny with photos on the walls of such things as Y Mountain, LaVell Edwards Stadium, the Marriott Center, and BYU's mascot Cosmo. Even the owners often asked, "When you live in New Jerusalem, why in the world would you be nostalgic for Provo?" But it remained a popular place to dine for the middle-aged couples in Zion.

As they were seated at their table and the waitress brought them mugs of root beer, they all smiled. "Whoa, this is like the Twilight Zone," Tad said. "How long has it been since we last got together in Provo? It feels like fifty years ago."

Josh laughed. "Believe it or not, it hasn't even been five years."

"That's crazy," Tad said. "Now you're an apostle, Doug is one of the 144,000, and I don't have the chip in my hand anymore."

They all laughed, knowing that despite the important positions held by the other men, Tad had been on a bigger personal roller coaster the past few years than any of them.

They had a fun evening as they updated each other on their children and some of the wild experiences that had gone through since they last went out together. Josh in particular enjoyed being able to have a normal night out with friends who had known him before he was a General Authority.

They talked about some of their friends and neighbors in Utah who had chosen not to join the Saints in the mountain camps, and how they had never been heard from again. Emma shared how she had searched the ZOOM website for many of her former ward members, but she hadn't found any of them. "I'm afraid they didn't survive," she said.

Doug nodded. "That really was a time of sifting within the Church. I can remember people at the time telling me that the Lord was asking too much of us to leave our houses and possessions. But looking back, I feel so blessed. Our lives here in Zion are better than I could have imagined."

They all agreed with him, and soon the conversation turned to the future. Tad told them the temple was nearly completed, and he loved being a part of the construction team.

"As you know, Josh and Kim, most of my co-workers are from the Guatemalan group you led here," Tad said. "They are fantastic workers, and their ideas and suggestions have helped our work on the temple go much more quickly. I'm so grateful for them."

"Thank you for saying that," Kim said. "Yes, they've blessed our lives in so many ways, and after seeing some of their ancestors' amazing ancient temples in Guatemala, it isn't so surprising that those skills have been passed down through the generations and put to good use here."

Tad added that he had been helping apply the gold plating to the 24 columns that would support the center spire, and soon the dome would be raised.

"I hope to be here to see that," Doug said, "but there's a chance I might not be."

"What do you mean?" Kim asked.

"Well, as one of the 144,000, I'm directed by the Spirit. I might wake up in the morning and feel prompted to go to Florida, and if that happened I would go. But right now I feel the Lord is letting me recharge my batteries and be here with Becky and the kids. It's been wonderful."

"So you feel you'll be leaving again soon?" Tad asked.

"I do. My assignment isn't over, and I'm not sure it ever will be until the Second Coming."

Tad then turned to Josh. "How about you? It seems like all the apostles have stayed here in Zion lately."

Josh frowned a little. "Deep down I think I'll be leaving again soon, too."

This was news to Kim. "Has the prophet said anything to you?" she asked.

He shook his head. "No, but there's important work for the apostles to do outside of Zion. It's just a matter of whether I'm given one of the assignments. Since I'm the only apostle with little kids, I'm hoping the Lord will keep me here close by, although that might be expecting too much. But we have been so blessed, and I have no right to complain."

They all were silent for a moment, knowing that despite their daily trials and challenging callings, the Lord had indeed greatly blessed them, and deep down they knew that if they could remain faithful, they would gain their eternal reward.

They soon headed for the door, and as they gave each other hugs good-bye, Josh said, "That was really great. Thanks to the wives for getting us together."

Emma smiled. "Thanks for coming! Let's not wait another five years for the next time."

# CHAPTER 13

In the weeks following Mathoni's assignment to help Josh Brown bring the ancient Nephite plates to New Jerusalem, he had fulfilled several other errands for the Lord. But he knew he needed to touch base with his close friend John the Beloved.

Mathoni thought about John and also about the two other translated Nephites who were working diligently to strengthen Zion. The four of them had gotten together quite often during the slow centuries of the Dark Ages, but ever since Joseph Smith's First Vision in 1820, all four of them had been constantly busy doing the work of the Lord with hardly a moment to rest.

The four men didn't have official assigned areas, but over the past two centuries, Mathoni had spent nearly all of his time in North America, while his Nephite brethren had divided up Central and South America. He knew the explosive growth of the Church there in recent decades could be partly attributed to their hard work. Meanwhile, John had focused on helping the Saints in Europe and Asia while also working often with the so-called Lost Ten Tribes.

As Mathoni pondered the growth of New Jerusalem and the timing of world events, he knew he couldn't put off his meeting with John any longer, so he knelt and prayed for guidance from the Spirit in locating his friend. After receiving an answer about John's location, he said to himself, "This should be interesting. I've always wanted to see a Siberian sunrise."

Mathoni then used his ability as a translated being to travel rapidly to any location on earth, vanishing from the Western Hemisphere.

✢ ✢ ✢

At that moment, John the Beloved stood upon the sacred mountain known as Tatar Haia in central Siberia. He smiled with satisfaction as he looked down at the forested cliffs along the mighty Lena River, the source of life for the Yakut people who lived in the towns and villages in the valleys below.

John had spent portions of the past two centuries in this part of Asia preparing this people for what awaited them. The Yakuts themselves didn't fully comprehend who they were—descendants of the Lost Ten Tribes with a glorious future in Zion. Their ancestors were those Israelites mentioned in the Bible that had been led to the north countries many years before the Savior's earthly mission. Some remnants of the tribes had made their way to Europe and the British Isles, but most of the tribes had found refuge here in the Siberian wilderness, raising herds of reindeer for food and living humbly in ancient log dwellings.

There were now nearly a million people of direct Israelite descent safely hidden within these forests, essentially ignored and unknown to most of the world. Scientists and scholars had begun to pay attention to the Yakuts, though. They had noticed the group's unusual genetic traits compared to other Siberian groups and theorized the Yakuts had come from a southern region near the Mediterranean Sea. Other hints of that origin were the depictions in their stories and artistic works of lions, camels, and other animals from the Middle East that had never been seen in Siberia.

John had first visited the Yakut people in the early 1830s after an inspiring visit with the prophet Joseph Smith in Kirtland, Ohio. John and Joseph had spent an afternoon discussing the importance of preparing the Lost Tribes to eventually receive the gospel, and John had left that same day to begin his work among them.

To John's surprise, that first year in Siberia had been quite challenging. As he began mingling among the people, he aroused suspicions, and several attempts were made to kill him—without success, of course. At that time the Yakuts were only a few years removed from a long civil war that had greatly reduced their numbers and had caused deep emotional scars among the people. Their form of religion was primitive at best, and they had long forgotten their true identity.

However, John had soon befriended a couple named Nikolai and Alexandra Yakovlevna, who the Lord had revealed to John as the key family in preparing the Ten Tribes for their eventual journey to New Jerusalem several generations later.

John had presented himself to the couple as a world traveler, and they enjoyed hearing his stories. He told them about other countries around the world, and he shared with them his "theory" that their people had originally lived in a land far to the south. Nikolai and Alexandra were very intrigued by that idea.

"That could be true," Nikolai had said. "Our people have the tradition that very long ago a chief named Elai, the son of a great leader in middle-Asia, led his people north and east until they reached the banks of the Lena River near the sacred mountain Tatar Haia. Elai carried with him the teachings of our people engraved on a stone tablet. When he saw the flowing waters of the river he flung the tablet in the water and told his followers to drop their saddle blankets. The Yakut had found the land they sought."

When John heard that story, he knew the couple would be open to learning more about their ancestors. John told them about the Israelites and the city of Jerusalem. He also told them about Jesus Christ and gave them a copy of the Bible. He encouraged them to read it, saying he would return in a few weeks. When he returned, they had both read it and were very excited because many of the stories in the Bible matched their own traditions, such as the worldwide flood. The story of Moses leading the Israelites out of Egypt closely followed another of their traditions. They also followed many of the teachings of the man known in the Bible as Jesus Christ.

John had been very busy in the British Isles in the late 1830s and early 1840s as the LDS apostles spread the gospel there and baptized thousands of converts, but he still stayed in contact with the Yakovlevna family every year or so. He always brought more copies of the Bible for them to share with their children, extended family members and neighbors, and slowly a band of Christians began to grow in the heart of Siberia. It had been a slow process over several decades, but John felt that most of the Yakut people were now ready to hear the fullness of the gospel.

✣ ✣ ✣

John was shaken out of his memories by the sudden presence of someone standing behind him on the sacred Siberian mountain.

"John, is that you?" a man asked.

John warily turned around before saying in surprise, "Mathoni! It's great to see you again."

"Well, I knew I needed to check in with you concerning the Ten Tribes," Mathoni said. "The big event isn't too far off."

"You're right," John said. "How has your training with Elder Brown been going?"

John knew that Mathoni had been given the special assignment of tutoring Elder Josh Brown, the man the Lord had chosen long ago in the premortal world to help lead the Lost Tribes to Zion.

Mathoni smiled as he thought of Josh. "He has done very well. At first, he went through those stages we all do as we fulfill our assignments—nervousness, insecurity, and so on. When I first started working with him, he was already in Guatemala as a successful mission president. Then suddenly he found himself as a General Authority and being asked to lead thousands of people to New Jerusalem. I could tell he was a bit overwhelmed, but he also had tremendous faith, and our journey was a great growing experience for him."

"Very good," John said. "The group he's about to lead is several times larger than that group from Guatemala, but it sounds like he'll be fine."

"Yes, he's a true leader, yet so humble," Mathoni said.

How is his other training going?" John asked. "We won't get too far without it."

Mathoni laughed. "As you might expect, he struggled a bit at first, but he is getting better at it. When we hid the busload of plates on the Hopi reservation, I purposely buried it under a large pile of rocks so that he would have to move them later. By the time he moved the last rocks, he was completely confident, and I know when the time comes, he'll succeed."

"That's excellent news," John said. "It sounds like I need to make a visit to the First Presidency."

"You're right. I think the day has finally arrived that we've waited for so long."

"Will you be able to join me?" John asked.

Mathoni shook his head. "I need to finish another assignment, but I'm glad I caught you. I'll be in touch."

The two servants of the Lord shared a brief handshake and then parted ways. Mathoni went to northern Mexico to help a group of Saints who had traveled to an abandoned LDS temple site in order to establish a city of Zion.

Meanwhile, John quickly found himself standing outside the Church Administration Building in New Jerusalem. He walked inside and introduced himself to the receptionist. She was a bit stunned, but she paged the prophet, who invited John to join him in his office.

# CHAPTER 14

Within half an hour, John the Revelator was standing with the First Presidency and the members of the Quorum of the Twelve in their main meeting room. John had participated in a meeting with the apostles in the Salt Lake Temple a few days before the Coalition invasion, so he had met all of the apostles except the newest ones, Elder Brown and Elder Negus.

Those two apostles shook hands with John, and Elder Negus said, "I've seen you somewhere before. You look so familiar."

John grinned. "You've got a good memory. I checked up on you a few times when you were a teenager living in England. You could've had a great career as a soccer goalie if the Lord hadn't had other things in mind for you."

Elder Negus' eyes grew big, and the other apostles chuckled. "Get used to it," the prophet told him. ""John seems to know more about me than I know about myself."

John then turned to Josh and pulled him close before whispering, "I heard the rock removal around the bus in Hopiland went smoothly. Good job."

"How do you know . . ." Josh started to say, but let it trail off as John patted him reassuringly on the arm. John then moved to the front of the room as the Church leaders took their seats.

"Thank you for making time for me today," John said. "I was in Siberia less than an hour ago looking down on a village of my dear friends, the Yakut people, who are descendants of the Lost Ten Tribes. Contrary to some of the crazy stories you may have heard over the years, the Ten Tribes aren't living on another planet or living inside the earth under the polar ice caps. They are alive and well in Siberia, and it is our obligation to bring them into the Church just like all the other scattered remnants of the tribes of Israel. However, we're going to do it in a slightly more spectacular fashion. I know the gentlemen in the First Presidency already know most of the story, but let me update the rest of you on the situation among them."

John then summarized his experiences in Siberia since the 1830s and explained his tutoring of the Yakovlevna family and their descendants through the years, including teaching them Christianity.

One apostle raised his hand. "John, I'm thrilled to hear that thousands of people there are Christians, but isn't the return of the Ten Tribes supposed to be a colossal event? Don't we expect almost all of them to pack their bags and come here to Zion?"

"Yes, we do," John said. "I expect there will be about a million people making the journey together."

The number seemed staggering to the apostles, and there was some whispering back and forth.

Another apostle spoke up. "John, please help me understand something. Why would these people leave their homeland to come here before they're even members of the Church?"

John nodded appreciatively. "That's a very interesting question. I feel the best comparison is with the spirit of Elijah that many people feel concerning family history work. They might not even know about temple work, but they feel driven to find their ancestors. Another more direct comparison is the yearning that many Jewish people feel to return to Israel. Although they don't consciously comprehend why they have that feeling, there's an inner drive to do so. I also know that as we teach the Yakuts about their true origins and what their future holds, they will eagerly journey to New Jerusalem."

The apostles all nodded, and another apostle raised his hand. "You seem to indicate the tribes are now gathered fairly close together, but earlier you made it sound like they were scattered over thousands of miles when you first started working among them. What did you do to get them back as a group?"

John smiled. "That's an excellent question, and to be honest, I didn't have much to do with gathering them together. It was one of those cosmic events set up by the Lord that worked perfectly. In early 1908 the Lord visited me and showed me a vision of a meteor that was heading toward earth. He told me it would explode over central Siberia. Millions of trees would be toppled, buildings would be destroyed, and anyone living within a certain area would be killed."

Several apostles were again nodding their heads. "I remember learning about that in school," one apostle said. "The 1908 Siberian Meteor Explosion."

"Exactly," John replied. "The Lord told me the meteor would serve to gather the people together in tighter communities and prepare them for their future journey to Zion. He also told me that he would send dreams to the Siberian religious leaders, known as shamans, that they should warn the people about the meteor. The Lord sent the dreams two months before the explosion, and the shamans began going from one settlement to another, telling the people of the upcoming cataclysm.

"The people might not have believed one or two shamans, but when *all* of them were spreading the same message, the people listened. They began to move their reindeer herds from the upper reaches of the region and traveled several hundred miles toward the Lena River. Also, the leaders of several nomadic clans agreed to move closer together. Curiously, even the wild animals also began to leave the area. The birds flew from their nesting grounds, the swans left the lakes and the fish disappeared from the rivers. So I was certain that the Lord in his own kind way had also warned the animals about what was going to happen."

The apostles were silent, pondering over the goodness of the Lord. John continued, "So on the morning of June 30, 1908, the meteor entered the earth's atmosphere. It was quite large, but it exploded in the air rather than directly hitting the ground. To help you understand how that impacted the area, the explosion was about 1,000 times as powerful as the bomb dropped on Hiroshima, Japan in World War II. As the Lord had warned, the explosion knocked over an estimated 80 million trees in a circular pattern away from the explosion point that covered nearly a thousand square miles. The shock wave knocked people off their feet and broke windows hundreds of miles away. The blast registered on seismic stations across the world, and over the next few weeks, night skies around the world were aglow from the dust suspended in the stratosphere by the explosion."

"Where were you at the time of the explosion?" one of the apostles asked.

John's eyes twinkled. "Oh, I wanted to see it up close, and it was an amazing sight, other than it literally blew me ten miles through the air. It was a rough landing, but it was quite a ride."

John then spent the next several minutes explaining how the meteor explosion was the turning point for all of the Yakut people, similar to how the Nephites responded after the destruction of their land following the Savior's crucifixion. The people began to recognize the hand of God in their lives, and the Siberian Christians made a more concentrated effort to share the gospel message, which boosted their numbers substantially.

When the Russians began to move farther into the area following the Revolution of 1917, it was a great boon for the Yakuts, because the Russians helped them build better cities and educate their children. But they also knew of the Soviet leaders' dislike for organized religion, so they kept secret their beliefs in Jesus Christ.

So for the past century the Lord had continually blessed the Yakuts. Many of their young people had attended the colleges the Russians had built, and they had learned English. They then taught the language to their families when they returned home, so the people were being quietly prepared for their great journey to Zion.

✢ ✢ ✢

Josh had been eagerly soaking in John's report. It all sounded so familiar to him, as if all of this information was already in his mind. But he could never have been more shocked than the words he heard next as John stepped aside to let the prophet speak.

"Thank you, John, for your report," the prophet said. "As you can see, brethren, the time has come for the Ten Tribes to be gathered to Zion. As you know, on April 3, 1836, Joseph Smith was visited in the Kirtland Temple by several resurrected beings, including the Savior himself. One of these visits came from the prophet Moses. Let me read to you how it is worded in Doctrine and Covenants 110:11."

The prophet opened up his scriptures and read, "*After this vision closed, the heavens were again opened unto us; and Moses appeared before us, and committed unto us the keys of the gathering of Israel from the four parts of the earth, and the leading of the ten tribes from the land of the north.*"

The prophet closed his scriptures and said, "Those same keys have been passed down to each president of the Church, and I now hold them. At this time I'm exercising those keys and authorizing Elder Joshua Brown to lead the Ten Tribes of Israel to New Jerusalem so they can be taught the gospel and receive the ordinances of the temple."

The prophet's words literally froze Josh in place. He felt like a giant weight had just crushed his chest. All eyes in the room were upon him.

"What did you just say?" he finally said softly.

John stepped toward him, took him by the hand and pulled him to his feet. "It's an immense task, but you've been prepared for it in many ways. Don't worry, I'll be by your side when you need help."

Josh smiled weakly. "Then I accept. It will be a privilege."

"Very good," the prophet said. "Arrangements have already been made for you to travel to Siberia."

Then a strong impression flashed through Josh's mind, and he felt compelled to tell the prophet about it.

"I don't really know why, but I feel I should bring along a young man I've known for several years. Some of you know him from his service in helping defeat the Coalition army—the young man from Bulgaria named Mitko Petrov."

The prophet pondered Josh's request, then said, "That feels right to me. Do you know where he is?"

"I believe he's in St. Louis helping the Saints arriving from the eastern European countries make the transition here."

"Let's send for him immediately," the prophet said. "I would like to give both of you a priesthood blessing before your departure."

A message was sent to Mitko and he was on his way, but it would take him a few hours to arrive. In the meantime, John and Josh spent some time discussing their upcoming assignment.

"How are we going to get to Siberia?" Josh asked. "Too bad we can't fly there."

"Well, we actually *are* taking a plane," John said. "I'll be flying us to a secret airstrip in Siberia."

Josh's eyes bulged a little. "Whoa. You're a pilot?"

"Yes. There is a plane ready for us at an abandoned airport in Kansas. It's actually a small private jet that was once owned by a wealthy member of the Church. It will get us there without any difficulties."

"I don't get it," Josh said. "Are you even allowed to fly?"

John laughed. "You're an apostle, but you still have interests outside of the Church, don't you?"

"Well, yes."

"So do I. Even though myself and the Three Nephites are translated beings, we still can pursue hobbies that will help further the Lord's work. For example, Mathoni really has a fascination with automobiles, and he has a car he keeps handy for assignments. You've ridden in his car, haven't you?"

"Yes, we drove it to Arizona."

"That's right. Anyway, I really like airplanes. Can you blame me? I'd been on the earth for 2,000 years with a horse and wagon being the main mode of transportation, and suddenly these huge machines are flying through the sky. So I took flying lessons, and it was really enjoyable to soar above the lands I had walked for so many years. Plus, it's a useful skill I've used many times to assist the First Presidency around the world. I was very happy when Elder Uchtdorf was made an apostle. He and I had some pretty good talks about aviation."

Josh shook his head. "I'm surprised you had to take flying lessons. Couldn't you just get in the cockpit and already know how to fly a plane?"

John laughed. "Even translated beings have to learn how to do things. We don't instantly know everything."

"That makes sense."

Josh stood up and stretched his legs. "I need to go home and tell Kim a little bit about where I'm going. I'll be back before Mitko arrives, but I want to spend some time with her and the twins before we leave."

"Absolutely," John said. "I was about to suggest that myself."

Josh pondered for a moment. "Will there really only be the three of us going?"

"Yes. There are hundreds of Yakut men who are prepared to help us on the journey once we get them organized. Our main purpose is to baptize their leaders and ordain them to the Melchizedek Priesthood so that they can be spiritually ready for the journey. I gave copies of the Book of Mormon to their village leaders a few years ago, and they are well-versed in basic LDS doctrine. Now they're very eager to join the Church."

"Then how come they haven't been baptized yet?" Josh asked.

"Part of it was a matter of timing," John said. "But another factor is I hold the priesthood, but I'm not a member of the latter-day Church. So I need an authorized servant there to perform the ordinances, and that's where you come in. It will snowball from there as those men take over and baptize their relatives and neighbors at a later time."

"That sounds great, "Josh said. "I still feel a bit overwhelmed, but I'm also getting very excited."

John suddenly became emotional. "I've waited so long for this day. It is going to be an amazing experience for everyone."

# CHAPTER 15

━━━━━━━━━━━ ✤ ━━━━━━━━━━━

Mitko Petrov's head was spinning a little as he looked out the window of the small private jet that was taking them northward. Dusk was settling upon them and stars were becoming visible. He looked over at Elder Brown, who was sleeping in the seat beside him. They had been friends ever since Mitko's mission in Nebraska several years earlier, where Elder Brown had been serving as a stake president. He had grown close to the Browns, and they had always been supportive of him, even after he returned to Bulgaria following his mission.

Although it hadn't been his wish, after his mission Mitko had become part of the Coalition forces that invaded America. In hindsight, he could now see the hand of the Lord placing him where he needed to be. As the war had rushed to a climax, Mitko had left the Coalition camp and provided key information to the Elders of Israel that allowed them to win the war.

When New Jerusalem was established, Mitko had helped for several months with the reconstruction of the city. However, as the Saints from Europe and Asia began arriving in New Orleans and then reaching St. Louis, Mitko's language skills were needed in helping process the new arrivals. So he had been serving in St. Louis ever since, and he had really enjoyed it. His supervisors thought he did a fantastic job dealing with people, and he expected to continue serving there until all of the Saints from overseas had arrived. So when the call had come that morning for him to leave immediately for New Jerusalem, it had come as a surprise.

After arriving back in the city, he had been whisked away by

Church security personnel to an abandoned airport in Kansas. By now he had been really confused, but it was a relief to see Elder Brown standing outside the jet. The apostle had told him they were flying to Asia on a crucial assignment, but he didn't share much more information. Mitko had briefly shaken hands with the pilot as they boarded the plane, but he hadn't left the cockpit since.

"I guess I'll just have to wait and see what is happening," Mitko told himself. He tried to sleep, but his mind was still racing.

Two hours later they landed at an isolated airfield outside of Cardston, Canada, where a solitary fueling truck was waiting for them. They all got out to stretch their legs, and a man with brown hair and blue eyes greeted them and filled the jet with fuel. Mitko noticed the man was wearing a T-shirt that read "*The Sons of Helaman Were Mommas Boys.*"

They were soon in the air again until landing in Anchorage, Alaska, where once again a fuel truck pulled alongside the plane. Out of the truck climbed a man wearing a shirt that read, "*My Body Is a Caffeine-Free Zone.*"

As they stood around waiting as the jet was fueled, Mitko whispered to Josh, "Doesn't he look a lot like that last fuel guy we met?"

The apostle smiled slightly. "You really think so? I guess there's a resemblance."

Then on their third refueling stop in eastern Siberia, the same routine took place. The fuel truck pulled up and out of the truck jumped that same familiar guy! Only this time he was wearing a shirt that showed Homer Simpson swordfighting Darth Vader with Chinese words beneath them. Josh pointed at the shirt and started chuckling, but the fuel guy just went about his business as if nothing was unusual.

Mitko was now nearly beside himself. "What's going on here? This guy has been at all of the refueling stops."

There were a few moments of awkward silence, then the

refueling man burst out laughing and stuck out his hand to Mitko. "Let me introduce myself. I'm Mathoni, one of the Three Nephites. Yes, I've been hopping ahead of you to keep your plane refueled. I thought I might as well have a little fun with you."

Mitko started laughing. "You certainly got me! I thought I was hallucinating."

The pilot then stuck out his hand as well. "Forgive me for being a little distant so far on the trip, but I felt that identifying myself would only create more questions in your mind. But we're nearly there, so it can't hurt. I'm John the Revelator, and we're on our way to lead the Lost Ten Tribes back to New Jerusalem."

Mitko turned to Josh and asked, "Is this really true?" The news almost sounded more unbelievable than Mathoni's prank had been.

Josh smiled and said, "Absolutely."

Mitko shook his head. "Wow, I feel a little overwhelmed, hanging out with an apostle and two translated beings."

Josh put his arm around his shoulder. "You're going to be fine. I assure you the Lord wants you on this assignment."

This would be their final refueling stop, so they bid farewell to Mathoni. As they prepared to board the jet, Josh pointed at Mathoni's swordfighting shirt and said, "You might as well destroy that ugly thing. It'll go up in flames at the Second Coming anyway."

"I'm sure it will," the Nephite said. "But I knew it would make you laugh."

❖   ❖   ❖

Once they were in the air again, Mitko decided to take a much-needed nap, so Josh joined John in the cockpit. As he settled into the co-pilot's seat, the sun was coming up behind them and the view was spectacular. Forests, lakes and mountains stretched all the way to the horizon.

"It's so . . . huge," Josh said.

"Siberia is an amazing place," John replied. "Now you can see why it really wasn't that difficult for the Lord to hide the Ten Tribes here."

They flew on in silence for a few moments. Josh looked over at John, who looked completely peaceful and seemed to radiate joy.

"I have a question," Josh said. "You and Mathoni are possibly the happiest people I've ever met. What's the story there?"

"Why shouldn't we be happy? We're doing the work of the Lord. Besides, Mathoni and I just really enjoy being around each other, and we've bonded over the centuries. Admittedly, the two other Nephites don't quite have Mathoni's sense of humor. They're much more serious."

Josh shrugged a little. "I guess I'm feeling the pressure of that old stereotype that I should be serious all the time—that it's sacrilegious to have a little fun if you're an apostle. For example, not long ago Kim and I went to dinner with some old friends, and as we reminisced about our younger days, I laughed so hard that it hurt. But then I felt a little guilty about it. Some other people in the restaurant saw me laughing, and from the looks on their faces I'm sure they didn't feel it was appropriate behavior for an apostle."

"I wouldn't worry about it," John said. "I've found that apostles are among the most joyful people on earth, and translated beings are even happier. It's like the joy gets magnified, and from what I can tell, when you're resurrected with a celestial body, you're practically giddy. Those people always have smiles on their faces. Do you know who is the happiest person I know?"

"The Savior?"

"That's right. He's delightful in every way. His laugh is infectious, and he taught me to enjoy life, so I do my best to do so."

John then changed the subject a little. "I don't want to dampen the mood, but I've certainly been through some challenging times, and you'll still face some troubles before your mortal life is over. But always keep your faith strong."

John paused as he remembered the darkest days of his life. "I don't think anyone really comprehends what the Savior's followers went through during the week of his crucifixion. We fully expected Jesus to establish an earthly kingdom and we would be rulers in it. Then the next thing we know he is taken away, beaten, and nailed to a cross. If ever there was a time to lose faith, that was it. I was standing helplessly in front of the cross, watching as each painful breath put pressure on the Savior's hands, arms, and feet. Oh, it was horrible. Some people say that it wasn't as bad for him, since he was the Son of God, but I assure you it was as excruciating for him as it would be for any man. Plus, at the same time he was suffering for the sins of the world. He was in intense agony, and it really felt like my heart was being ripped out as I watched him suffer. It isn't an understatement to say the whole universe grieved for its Creator that day."

Josh shook his head slowly, picturing the scene in his mind. "But then the Lord asked you to care for his mother . . ."

"Yes. Mary was as grief-stricken as anyone I've ever seen. She had raised the Son of God, yet now he was being crucified. All of us were overwhelmed and confused, but it had to be that way so that the Savior could truly descend below all things. However, as dark as those days were for us following his death, nothing could compare to the joy we felt when he appeared to us and we were able to touch his resurrected body. He explained why everything had happened the way it did, and the gospel plan suddenly fit together completely in my mind. That's why I asked him if I could stay on the earth and spread the gospel message until he comes again. I've never regretted that decision, and I hope I can always serve him with all of my heart."

Josh felt a rush of emotion and put his hand on John's shoulder. "Thank you so much. I'll never forget this conversation. You're an amazing man."

John shook his head. "I'm really not. I've just sought to keep the Lord's commandments and help other people. I hope my small efforts are an acceptable offering to the Lord."

# CHAPTER 16

Jeremiah Yakovlevna stood alone on the empty airstrip outside the city of Yakutsk, Siberia watching the sky for any sign of an airplane. He blew on his hands and stomped his feet to fight off the chill. His friend John had left a note on his door two days earlier that he would be landing a plane at the airport at this time and he needed Jeremiah to pick him up.

Jeremiah had been a bit skeptical about the request, partly because a plane hadn't arrived at this airport in at least three years. However, he knew John's true identity as a translated being, so anything was possible. Deep down, Jeremiah knew the only reason John would need a plane was if he was bringing someone else with him.

"Maybe the appointed day is finally here," Jeremiah said to himself. "It can't be much longer."

Jeremiah was a great-great-grandson of Nikolai and Alexandra Yakovlevna, the couple who John the Revelator had first made contact with in the 1830s. Over time, John had helped the Yakovlevna family understand that they were descended from the Lost Ten Tribes, and he told them they were members of the Israelite tribe of Issachar.

John greatly admired Jeremiah, in large part because the fun-loving, humble Siberian didn't fully understand what a splendid, talented person he was. John had carefully watched the descendants of Nikolai for decades, and at last a true leader had been born that would have the leadership skills to lead the tribes to New Jerusalem. There had been other men among the tribes who had been successful leaders, but Jeremiah was a unique mixture of Joseph Smith, David O. McKay and Steve Young. He had a dynamic personality and was gentle and teachable—yet he was as strong and smart as a Hall of Fame NFL quarterback.

Jeremiah's parents had died in a sleigh accident when he was only ten years old, but their deaths made him grow emotionally and spiritually. He had never blamed God for their deaths. They had taught him their Christian beliefs, and he knew his parents were now in a better place in the Spirit World.

Jeremiah had lived with relatives until he was 15, but then he had moved back into the family home, which had been vacant since his parents' death. No one argued with his decision to return to the house. After all, it was his home and had been handed down from father to son for centuries.

John had sought him out while he was a teenager, and Jeremiah had eagerly accepted John's teachings. He hungered to be baptized into the Savior's true church. Because of his spiritual maturity and understanding of the Bible, Jeremiah was the first person among the tribes that John revealed his true nature as a translated being, and they had developed a tight bond. John had shared with him many insights hidden within the Book of Revelation, and clarified how future events would relate to his people.

With John's encouragement, Jeremiah had attended a university in the modern city of Yakutsk for a year just before the world was thrown into commotion because of the Coalition invasion of the United States. During that year Jeremiah had learned many things about the world and modern society through his classes. He had also strengthened his English skills, knowing they would likely come in handy in the future.

He also soaked in everything he could from the internet about the Church. The website www.lds.org was a site he visited often, and he had read all of the General Conference talks going back to the 1980s. His yearning to become a member was like a constant gnawing in his soul, and once he had actually sat in the school library and typed an e-mail to Church headquarters that read, "*My name is Jeremiah Yakovlevna, and John the Revelator is preparing me to help lead the Lost Ten Tribes to New Jerusalem. It won't be for several years, but I just wanted you to know that I greatly desire to be a member of the Church.*"

He added several more sentences, including his hometown. As he read through it a second time, a person was suddenly looking over his shoulder. "Hit the delete button," John told him quietly but firmly. "It isn't part of the Lord's plan to have the location of the Ten Tribes be revealed to the world by e-mail."

Jeremiah blushed, then quickly deleted the message. He turned around and said, "I knew it wasn't right, but I feel so alone. I'm ready to be a member of Christ's true church. Why can't I just go to Moscow and get baptized by the missionaries there? What would it hurt?"

John smiled slightly. "I understand your feelings, but please keep the big picture in mind. I've seen the day of your baptism, and it will be marvelous. You'll set a great example to your people, and which will motivate hundreds of others to be baptized that same day as well."

"I can hardly imagine that," Jeremiah said, his eyes getting a little misty.

"Don't worry," John said, "all of the blessings of the gospel, including the temple ordinances, will be available to you soon enough. So can I trust you to keep your people hidden from the world for a while longer?"

"Yes. I'll just focus on helping my own people learn more about the gospel."

And in the intervening years since that day, Jeremiah had kept his word. Once the war started, he had returned to his village and had personally taught dozens of families about their true Israelite heritage and the Lord's eternal plan for them. He would also teach them from the Book of Mormon, particularly about the Savior's visit to the Nephites.

As part of his lessons, he would read to them Third Nephi 17:4, which reads: "*But now I go unto the Father, and also unto the lost tribes of Israel, for they are not lost unto the Father, for he knoweth whither he hath taken them.*"

Then Jeremiah would say to them, "I know Jesus visited our ancestors. We've all heard the traditions of the great god who brought peace to our people many years ago. I believe this god was Jesus Christ, and I know he's going to return again soon."

At that moment the Spirit would be very strong in the room, and the people couldn't deny the truthfulness of it. Jeremiah estimated that more than a thousand people would be baptized as soon as the opportunity was available, with several thousand more ready to follow.

One of the best things Jeremiah ever did was marry Tasha, a beautiful brunette who also had a strong testimony of the gospel. They had met soon after he returned from the university, and they had been inseparable ever since.

They often would go as a couple to teach other families about the gospel, and her testimony had a particular effect on the women they taught. Within a few months of their marriage, John shared with her his true identity, and she became even more stalwart in her faith.

Jeremiah and Tasha had one son, and they had named him Peter, after John's friend who had served as president of Christ's church in Jerusalem. John had told them many stories of Peter's courage and perseverance, and the couple hoped their son could be as devoted to living the gospel as his namesake had been. Peter was now nearly three years old, and he was full of energy and laughter that brightened his parents' lives.

After so many years of teaching the gospel, the prophecies concerning his people were imprinted on Jeremiah's mind, and he found himself repeating them whenever he had a quiet moment to reflect on these upcoming events. The scripture passage that he loved the most was found in D&C 133:26-34, and as he continued to wait for the plane, he rehearsed it in his head once again:

*"And they who are in the north countries shall come in remembrance before the Lord; and their prophets shall hear his voice, and shall no longer stay themselves; and they shall smite the rocks, and the ice shall flow down at their presence.*

*"And an highway shall be cast up in the midst of the great deep.*

*"Their enemies shall become a prey unto them,*

*"And in the barren deserts there shall come forth pools of living water; and the parched ground shall no longer be a thirsty land.*

*"And they shall bring forth their rich treasures unto the children of Ephraim, my servants.*

*"And the boundaries of the everlasting hills shall tremble at their presence.*

*"And there shall they fall down and be crowned with glory, even in Zion, by the hands of the servants of the Lord, even the children of Ephraim.*

*"And they shall be filled with songs of everlasting joy.*

*"Behold, this is the blessing of the everlasting God upon the tribes of Israel."*

The promises were so profound that Jeremiah would be content if even half of those events took place, but John had assured him that *all* of them would happen. John had told him the prophecies would begin to unfold with the arrival of a latter-day apostle in Siberia to set everything in motion.

"There *has* to be an apostle on this plane," Jeremiah muttered.

Twenty minutes later, Jeremiah breathed a sigh of relief as at last a small plane became visible on the eastern horizon and approached the airport. He stepped away from the side of the building where he had been sheltered from the wind and began waving his arms as the jet landed. It rolled to a stop within fifty yards of him. The door popped open and three men stepped out, including one with the familiar profile of John.

The men walked quickly toward him, and John gave him a big handshake. Then he motioned to the older of the two men and said, "Jeremiah, this is Elder Joshua Brown of the Quorum of the Twelve Apostles."

Jeremiah eagerly shook hands with Josh. "I've waited so long to meet an apostle of the Lord. Thank you for coming."

John then motioned for Mitko to step forward. "Please meet Mitko Petrov, a Melchizedek Priesthood holder who will be assisting us in our assignments."

Mitko smiled and told Jeremiah, "Maybe we're cousins. I was born on this continent as well. I'm originally from Bulgaria."

"It's a pleasure to meet you," Jeremiah said.

Just then a frigid gust of wind swept across the runway, causing the visitors to hunch down against the biting cold.

"Summer's coming, but it hasn't quite arrived here yet," Jeremiah said. "Let's get someplace warmer."

Jeremiah had driven to the airport in a four-seat snow machine, and he drove it near the plane and helped load in some luggage that the men had brought with them. Then the three mortals hopped in the machine to get out of the cold as John drove the plane to an abandoned hanger.

As they waited, Josh told Jeremiah, "During the flight here, John told me much about you. I know it's been a long wait for you to be baptized, but we'll take care of that as soon as we can."

Another gust of icy wind shook the machine, and Jeremiah smiled. "I can wait at least until tomorrow. I'd rather not freeze to death as soon as I came out of the water!"

# CHAPTER 17

The drive to Jeremiah's village in the snow machine was noisy and somewhat treacherous as night fell. Even though summer was approaching, a recent storm had blanketed the area with two feet of snow. As they moved away from the city into the rural landscape, the roads were often covered with snow drifts that the headlights often didn't reveal until the last moment.

Nearly three hours later Jeremiah turned off the main road and down a narrow lane. He soon pulled into a cluster of small log houses, all lined in neat rows. Each house had a steep roof and tiny windows, with a rock chimney at one end. Josh sensed they had been there for centuries. Most of them even tilted a little, as if they had actually sunk into the permafrost. Several lanterns had been lit along the street, and at the sound of the machine, a few doors had cracked open.

"We're finally here," Jeremiah said tiredly as he turned off the machine. "I hope everyone is still awake. I may have let it slip that I thought John might be bringing priesthood holders with him."

They got out of the machine and went to a large building in the center of the cluster of homes. Jeremiah turned to them and said, "I suppose you would call this our town hall. It's where we gather for important events. Most of my extended family should be here. They're eager to meet you."

As they opened the door, several people turned to look at them, and a cheer went up from the group. Jeremiah led the men to a small platform and he introduced them to the group.

"Most of you know my friend John, who has visited us for

many years," Jeremiah said. "He has brought with him Elder Joshua Brown, an apostle in the Church of Jesus Christ of Latter-day Saints, and Mitko Petrov, who holds the Melchizedek Priesthood. The day we have waited for has arrived. These men are authorized to baptize us into the Church of Jesus Christ!"

A buzz of excitement raced through the group, and a man called out, "When? Tonight?"

Josh laughed and told the group, "No, but pray for good weather tomorrow, and we'll see what we can do."

The group cheered, and then the men were led to a table where a feast of reindeer steaks and other delicacies were placed before them. It had been nearly thirty hours since they departed from Kansas, and the only food they had eaten in that time had been some supplies on the plane. John wasn't feeling too hungry, of course, but Josh and Mitko ate heartily. The food was delicious and it was hard to resist stuffing themselves.

As they finished their meal, a beautiful brunette approached them. "Hello, my name is Tasha Yakovlevna. I'm Jeremiah's wife. Thank you for coming all this way."

She then sat at their table and told them about her eagerness to join the Church and make the journey to New Jerusalem. "It sounds so wonderful. Do you really think we can hold the baptisms tomorrow?"

Josh hesitated. "My only concern is the weather. I don't want us all to catch cold."

Tasha laughed. "Don't worry. We've got that all figured out. We have a hot spring nearby that will work perfectly for us."

Mitko smiled at Josh. "Sounds good to me!"

The next morning was relatively warm and sunny, and everyone was in good spirits. Following a wonderful breakfast in the town hall, Josh, Mitko and Jeremiah led hundreds of people toward the hot spring.

Mitko looked around. "Where's John?"

"He told me he'd return in a few days," Josh said. "It sounded like he was going to other villages in Siberia he has been working with to tell them what is happening."

Josh and Mitko had worked out the details of performing the ordinances with Jeremiah and a few other men earlier that morning, since it was clear that hundreds—if not thousands—of baptisms would be performed. It was important that accurate records be kept of every baptism and confirmation, and that everyone's personal information was written down correctly. Josh also felt it was important for each person to receive a short interview. Jeremiah assured him that he could vouch for all of the people wanting to be baptized that day, but Josh still felt an obligation to look each person in the eye and gauge their gospel knowledge.

There had been two large tents set up. The first one was where the people would fill out their information and be interviewed by Josh. They would proceed from there to a line at the edge of the spring, where they would be baptized in the clothes they came in. They would then exit the water and go into another tent where they would dry off and then be confirmed a member of the Church. Josh worried a little that the people might feel it was like an assembly line, but Jeremiah assured him that no one would mind.

But those details could be worked out later. At the moment, everyone was awaiting the first baptism of the day. The spring was bordered on two sides by grassy slopes, and the crowd squeezed together to witness this historic occasion among their people.

Josh scanned the crowd and estimated that there were close to a thousand people sitting on the slopes. They were of all ages and sizes, but they all shared one thing in common—the light of Christ radiated in their eyes.

Josh smiled at Jeremiah, who stood next to him along the edge of the water. "John told me he had to convince you to wait to be baptized, but he promised you it would be worth it. Was he right?"

Jeremiah's eyes filled briefly with tears. "Yes, in every way."

"Then let's not make you wait any longer."

The two men waded out into the spring until the water was just above their waists, and the crowd grew silent, watching closely. Jeremiah took hold of Josh's left wrist with his right hand, just as they had practiced, and plugged his nose with the other hand. During their practice session, Jeremiah had tried to argue that he didn't need to plug his nose, but Josh had reminded him he was setting the example for everyone else, and it would be best to do it that way.

Once Josh had his feet set in the bottom of the spring, he raised his right arm to the square and said loudly, "Jeremiah Yakovlevna, having been commissioned of Jesus Christ, I baptize you in the name of the Father, and of the Son, and of the Holy Ghost. Amen."

Josh then smoothly lowered Jeremiah backward into the water, making sure he was completely submerged. He also looked over at Mitko on the shore to verify everything had been done properly. Once Mitko nodded, Josh pulled Jeremiah quickly from the water, causing a large ripple. Jeremiah's grin seemed to fill his entire face as he emerged, and the two men briefly patted each other on the back.

The crowd instantly was buzzing with excitement. The Spirit of the Lord was tangible, and Mitko looked around, half expecting angels to have appeared. He couldn't see any, but he certainly felt them nearby.

Josh and Jeremiah exited the water and quickly dried off the best they could. Then Jeremiah sat in a chair that had been placed on the bank. The crowd quieted again, and Mitko and Josh stood behind him and placed their hands on his head. Mitko cleared his throat and said, "Jeremiah Yakovlevna, by the power of the holy Melchizedek Priesthood which we hold, we confirm you a member of the Church of Jesus Christ of Latter-day Saints and say unto you, receive the Holy Ghost. Amen."

Both Josh and Mitko felt a surge of the Spirit pass through their arms as the words were being said, and Jeremiah also felt a strengthening power pass through him. The men removed their hands and Josh told Jeremiah, "Stay there. We have one more item of business, and then you'll be ready to help us. The Church policy is that a man must be worthy and at least 18 years of age to receive the Melchizedek Priesthood. Although it is standard procedure for a man to hold the Aaronic Priesthood first, it isn't a requirement. I feel impressed that because of your gospel knowledge and preparation, you should receive the Melchizedek Priesthood at this time."

"Thank you," Jeremiah said humbly. "I feel honored that you feel that way."

Josh and Mitko put their hands on Jeremiah's head once again, and Josh conferred upon him the Melchizedek Priesthood and ordained him to the office of an elder.

Once the ordination was complete, Josh told him, "You're now authorized to perform baptisms and confirmations. Is there anyone in particular who you would like to baptize first?"

Suddenly Tasha came running toward them. "I think there's your answer," Jeremiah said with a smile.

Following Tasha's baptism and confirmation, it took a few minutes to get organized. In order to have enough priesthood holders participating, they baptized and confirmed one of Jeremiah's closest friends, and then ordained him to the Melchizedek Priesthood so that he could assist Mitko with the confirmations. Then Josh began the interviews in the first tent, and soon everything was moving like clockwork. Jeremiah would perform the baptisms and Mitko would then confirm them in the second tent.

The person would simply state his or her name before being baptized or confirmed, and then the ordinances would be performed. Both Jeremiah and Mitko felt the sustaining influence of the Lord in helping them with their tasks, and even after two hours they didn't feel overly fatigued. Josh was concerned about Jeremiah's back muscles from the rigors of baptizing so many people in such a short amount of time, but nothing anyone said was going to get him out of the water. He'd waited too long for this day, and his adrenalin had certainly kicked in.

By noon they had baptized and confirmed more than two hundred people. During a break for lunch, Jeremiah admitted his back could use a rest, so Josh ordained additional men to the Melchizedek Priesthood so they could help both Jeremiah and Mitko. The men continued their work into the late afternoon, baptizing and confirming nearly a thousand people that day.

That evening a huge feast was held, and Josh spoke to the group for a few minutes. He told them how impressed he had been as he had interviewed them, and that they were truly prepared to be members of Christ's church.

He then said, "I am authorized as an apostle of Jesus Christ to organize this group into a ward of the Church of Jesus Christ of Latter-day Saints. A few minutes ago I called someone to serve as your bishop, and I now ask for your sustaining vote. Please raise your right hand if you are willing to sustain and support Brother Jeremiah Yakovlevna as the bishop of your ward."

All of the hands in the building enthusiastically went up, and Josh thanked them. "I will then proceed to ordain Brother Yakovlevna to the Melchizedek Priesthood and the office of high priest, and I'll also ordain him to the office of bishop."

Josh asked Jeremiah to take a seat at the front of the room and then he performed the ordination. Afterward, Josh gave him a congratulatory hug and then chuckled as he told the group, "For most men, it takes about 40 years to go from being baptized to becoming a bishop. Jeremiah has made the jump in about ten hours. That has to be some sort of record!"

Josh then explained the significance of the sacrament ordinance to the group, as Mitko prepared bread and water to be passed. The two men then offered the sacrament prayers as several newly ordained Aaronic Priesthood holders passed the sacrament to the people in attendance. It took awhile for everyone to receive it, but no one minded as they basked in the wonderful spirit that had filled the room. Afterward, the meeting developed into an impromptu testimony meeting, and the Holy Ghost testified to these new members of the truthfulness of the gospel.

The next few days were exciting as Josh and Mitko helped Jeremiah organize the group into a ward, complete with a full bishopric, and presidencies in the Elders Quorum, Primary, Relief Society, and the youth groups. They also ordained dozens of men as elders in the Melchizedek Priesthood and the teenage boys to the appropriate offices in the Aaronic Priesthood.

Josh hadn't heard from John, so he and Mitko spent each day training these new leaders in their duties. Everyone in this newly formed ward was exceedingly inexperienced, but Mitko noted that in some ways it wasn't a bad thing. They were pure-hearted and eager to serve their fellow ward members.

John returned to the village about two weeks after the baptisms had taken place, and he asked Josh, Jeremiah and Mitko to meet with him. He first congratulated Jeremiah on his new calling as the group's spiritual leader and listened happily as they reported on the success they'd experienced and how well these new Saints were eagerly serving one another.

"That's wonderful," John said. "Your success ties into what I've been doing these past few days. I've been spreading the word among the other remnants of the tribe of Israel here in Siberia that a great day is coming. I've told them a large group of people will be passing through their area on their way to live in the holy city known as New Jerusalem. I've worked with the people in these communities over the past several decades, and most of them at least believe in Christ and have some concept of being a Saint. Now that the seeds are planted, I'm confident they'll join you on the journey to Zion."

Jeremiah frowned. "Do we have to baptize them as we go? That could really slow us down."

John laughed. "No, that would be quite a task, since I'll bet you'll have a million people join you along the way. They won't really understand their compulsion to join you, but it's their spirits recognizing an agreement they made in the premortal world to do so. We'll get these people to Zion, and then let the Saints there do the missionary work and perform the baptisms."

"Then what's our next step?" Mitko asked.

"It's time to make our final preparations for our journey. Our timing is nearly perfect. The summer weather will make the trip across Siberia less difficult."

John turned to Jeremiah and said, "Bishop Yakovlevna, please have Elder Brown help you organize your ward into family groups with a leader in charge of each group. These will essentially be the traveling parties, so make them a workable number of around seventy people in each group. Then call other men to be in charge of seven groups each, who will report directly to Elder Brown if needed."

Jeremiah nodded. "So we're basically organizing ourselves like the Church does with wards, stakes, regions, and so on."

"Exactly," John said. "This won't be too difficult with the thousand or so Saints we're starting off with, but it will make the journey easier to manage when we start adding people to the group along the way."

Within a week, everyone was ready to go. The people weren't really taking many possessions with them, and each group had a main wagon pulled by two domesticated reindeer. It was quite a sight for Josh and Mitko who were so used to Santa Claus stories, but to everyone else having reindeer around was as perfectly natural as seeing a herd of horses in America.

Their departure was set for the following day, and everyone was eager to go. The group would be angling to the northeast toward the small ocean gap between Siberia and Alaska known as the Bering Strait. They had outlined a detailed route by using the best maps and guidebooks available, combined with the knowledge of the men in the group who had previously traveled throughout that area. It appeared there would usually be rivers or small roads to travel along, but in some areas the group might simply be walking across the open tundra.

A few of the people asked Jeremiah what the plan was for the tribes once they reached the ocean. "Are boats waiting there to take us across the sea?" they would ask.

Jeremiah would shrug and simply say, "I don't really know. From this point on, everything is in the Lord's hands."

# CHAPTER 18

On the night before their departure, Jeremiah had a nagging concern. He had meant to talk to John about it earlier, but it had been pushed to the back of his mind because of all the other exciting events that were taking place.

He had recently been drawn to a passage found in the Book of Mormon. He had read it before, but this time it struck him like a thunderbolt. It was in Second Nephi 19:12-13 and the Lord was teaching the prophet Nephi about the latter days. The Lord said:

*"For behold, I shall speak unto the Jews and they shall write it; and I shall also speak unto the Nephites and they shall write it; and I shall also speak unto the other tribes of Israel, which I have led away, and they shall write it; and I shall also speak unto all nations of the earth and they shall write it.*

*"And it shall come to pass that the Jews shall have the words of the Nephites, and the Nephites shall have the words of the Jews; and the Nephites and the Jews shall have the words of the lost tribes of Israel; and the lost tribes of Israel shall have the words of the Nephites and the Jews."*

Jeremiah loved these verses, but what bothered him was he felt his people weren't holding up their part of the bargain. He had held in his hands the Holy Bible—the record of the Jews—and the Book of Mormon, the record of the Nephites. But where were the records of his people?

He initially wondered whether someone else had them in their possession, but it was becoming obvious that he had been selected as the leader of this group, and he certainly didn't know where the records of the lost tribes were. That evening Jeremiah took John aside and shared his concern. John smiled, grateful that the Spirit had prompted Jeremiah to ask him about the records.

"Jeremiah, do you know why I contacted your great-great-grandfather in the first place back in the 1830s?"

"I have no idea."

"It was because the Lord had revealed to me that your family members were the guardians of the sacred records," John said. "The records have been passed down from father to son in your family since the time of Christ's visit among them soon after his resurrection."

Jeremiah was stunned by this news. "Then how come I never knew about them?"

"I suppose your father intended to tell you when you got older, but he died when you were very young and so he never got the chance."

Jeremiah was quiet for a moment, letting his mind search for any memories that could be tied to the records.

"I do remember a few things my father told me," he finally said. "He said our people had records that told of the visit of the great god of heaven, but that through the centuries the original language had been lost."

"That's right," John said. "Did he tell you anything else?"

"Yes, he said the tribal tradition was that a great prophet would someday translate them."

John patted him on the shoulder. "It sounds like your father had been slowly preparing you to be the next guardian of the records."

Jeremiah was truly disappointed. "It's a shame I never knew it was my responsibility."

"What do you mean? You've been the keeper of the records without even knowing it."

"I don't understand," Jeremiah said.

"The plates are hidden in your home," John said. "Your father would have eventually showed you where they are. Thankfully, he showed me the year before he died."

They hurried to the house, where Tasha was gently rocking Peter. "Shh," she whispered as they came in. "He's almost asleep."

"We'll be quiet," Jeremiah assured her as John went to the chimney on the far side of the room. As Jeremiah lit a lantern, John dislodged a large stone at the chimney base and revealed a small compartment.

"Go ahead and reach in there," he told Jeremiah. "After all, you're the guardian of the records."

Tasha was now quite intrigued and came over to watch, still holding Peter in her arms. Jeremiah reached into the compartment and pulled out a set of metal plates about the size of a Triple Combination. He showed them to his wife and said, "Apparently I've been guarding these since my father's death."

"There should be a total of three sets," John said.

Jeremiah reached deeper into the compartment and found the other two sets. They had been carefully wrapped in cloth, and they glistened in the light of the lantern.

"What do you think is written on them?" Tasha asked.

"I'm sure they contain the record of the Savior's visit among our people," Jeremiah said, looking at the strange writing on the plates. "But I know the prophet will be able to translate them. We'll pack them carefully and take them with us to Zion."

⚜ ⚜ ⚜

Meanwhile, at that same moment, Josh Brown was taking a quiet walk alone in the Siberian forest outside of the village. After the hectic past few days, he just needed to clear his head and contemplate what lay ahead on the journey to Zion. He knew he still had some major tasks to complete, and he planned to pray for heavenly help and guidance to accomplish them.

He soon saw a spot where he could kneel and pour out his heart to Heavenly Father, but as he sunk to his knees, he saw a figure leaning against a nearby tree. Josh quickly stood up and said, "Sorry to intrude. I thought I was alone out here."

"You *are* alone out here, Josh. Just you and me."

The figure moved closer, and Josh recoiled. He hadn't seen that face since he'd been in Guatemala. In a strange way, he wasn't too surprised to see his visitor. He seemed to show up at crucial moments in the earth's history, and the return of the lost tribes was certainly one of them.

"What's wrong, Josh?" Satan asked. "Are you nervous because you don't have John or Mathoni here to protect you? They've sure been at your side a lot lately. Don't I deserve equal time?"

"Satan, stay back," Josh said. "I don't want anything to do with you. I made that clear in Guatemala."

Satan laughed. "Are you talking about that wrestling match we had there along the highway? I want to apologize to you for that. I let my temper get the best of me."

"You would have killed me if Mathoni hadn't intervened," Josh said. "I have nothing to say to you."

"I wish you could remember how close we once were," Satan said quickly, trying to find some angle to keep Josh talking. "We had a great friendship in the premortal realm."

"You and me? I don't think so. I know you fought against Father's plan, and I'm sure I felt about you then as I do now."

Satan's calm demeanor cracked slightly. "Look at yourself! You think you're so powerful—an *apostle*. But I can give you so much more. What would you like? I can make you a ruler over all of Europe if you want, with riches beyond your wildest dreams . . ."

Satan didn't seem to realize he wasn't tempting Josh—only annoying him. "No thanks, Satan. Here's a question for you, though. Why don't you just give up? The battle is nearly over for you."

Satan acted like Josh had just slapped him in the face. "Why should I give up? I'm the one in control. Other than a few of your so-called cities of Zion, I rule the entire world!"

Josh shook his head in amazement at how deluded Satan was. "Surely you know that you have no chance of winning. Outer darkness is your ultimate destiny."

"That's a lie," Satan said angrily. "I will triumph! At this moment my servants are regrouping. Your little army may have fooled them in Denver, but there's no way you'll be able to fight off the millions of soldiers that will crush the so-called 'chosen ones' in Jerusalem. Then the world will be mine forever."

Josh realized that Satan had just told him more truth than he had intended. It was clear he was inspiring the evil men of the world to plan a massacre in Jerusalem of unthinkable proportions.

"Please don't do it," Josh said, showing a sense of compassion for the human race that Satan could never understand.

"Then join me," Satan said, growing confident. "If you help me, I'll call off the armies and together we can rule the world."

Josh regained his composure and said firmly, "You're a liar from the beginning. In the name of Jesus Christ, I command you to depart!"

Satan quickly disappeared, but his haunting laugh rang through the trees for several more seconds.

Following his disturbing encounter with Satan, Josh did finally kneel in prayer, and soon his soul was filled with a warm, comforting feeling. He hated dealing with Satan face-to-face, but he knew that standing for righteousness as a special witness of Jesus Christ meant he had to deal with the Evil One at times as well.

As he completed his prayer, Josh's mind was enlightened by the Lord of how Satan's plans could be disrupted. He hurried back to their sleeping quarters in the town hall and woke up Mitko, who had just gone to sleep.

"I now understand why you were sent here with me," Josh told him. "I was just visited by Satan, and he hinted that the Coalition forces have regrouped and are planning to annihilate Jerusalem."

"Did you say *Satan* visited you?"

"Yes, the old serpent himself. He never gives up. Anyway, after he departed, I prayed and received a strong prompting that you need to go west to infiltrate the Coalition leadership and learn their plans. The scriptures are filled with prophecies of the so-called

Armageddon at Jerusalem, but I had hoped it was still several years away. Hopefully you'll be able to forewarn us of their intentions. I'm not sure how we'll stay in contact, but we'll find a way."

Mitko was clearly nervous about the assignment, but he tried to lighten the mood by saying, "Does this make me a double-double agent? I'm losing track."

"All I know is that you've been guided by the Lord in every aspect of your life, and he'll help you on this mission as well."

Mitko nodded. "Do you have any suggestions on how I should present myself?"

"There's no reason to lie," Josh said. "Simply tell them that you were part of the Coalition forces, and that you survived the final battle in America. You've now traveled around the world to get back home."

"That really is the truth," Mitko said. "Where do you think I should go first?"

"I'm sure as you travel along, the citizens will be able to direct you to the Coalition headquarters, but I'd recommend heading toward Moscow, Russia."

"I'll bet you're right," Mitko said. "That will be my first destination."

So the next morning as the tribes began their journey east toward Zion, Mitko began his own journey west, heading into the unknown.

# CHAPTER 19

The Lord blessed the Ten Tribes in many ways as they made their journey eastward toward Siberia's northeast corner, where they planned to cross over to North America. Josh and Jeremiah were in the lead party, which included a dozen scouts that were constantly monitoring the path ahead. Six scouts at a time would travel in reindeer sleighs several miles ahead and then return to report their findings, at which time the next group would depart. Their efforts helped the group avoid washed-out bridges and landslides, and for the most part the journey had been free from major problems.

The weather had been fabulous, staying sunny with temperatures in the mid-70s during the day and staying well above freezing at night. Thankfully, keeping everyone fed hadn't been a problem, because the group's large reindeer herds had willingly been driven along behind the travelers.

As John had told them would happen, they met entire villages of people along the way that wanted to join them, which greatly added to their numbers. These people couldn't really explain why they wanted to abandon their homes, but they felt compelled to do so. They mentioned that a man named John had recently visited their village, and his message had been very convincing that they were members of the lost Ten Tribes who were meant to travel to New Jerusalem.

John had promised them that a large group would soon be passing by, and that they should join it. Many of these people had taken a wait-and-see approach, saying that if a large group really did come, then it was God's will that they join them. When they group arrived, that's exactly what they did, grabbing a few possessions and food supplies and marching away from their homes.

Once a village had joined the group, priesthood holders were assigned to supervise them, but for the most part the people who had been their village leaders simply continued in those roles, and family groups watched out for each other.

A curious part of the journey was that although the group's scouting party would report to Josh that there was ice on the roadway in the higher mountain passes, by the time the group reached that area the ice would have melted away, keeping the roadway dry and providing small streams of water along the edges of the road for the people to drink.

"It seems like a miracle," Josh once told Jeremiah as they walked along at the front of the immense group and watched a sheet of ice on the road ahead of them literally melt away before their eyes.

"Of course it's a miracle," Jeremiah responded. Then he quoted D&C 133 concerning the return of the Ten Tribes, "*. . . and the ice shall flow down at their presence.*"

Josh nodded gratefully. "The Lord truly is opening the way for us to reach Zion."

Later that day as they reached the top of yet another mountain pass, they turned and looked back at the group. It was an amazing sight. For as far as they could see the road through the mountains was filled with members of the Ten Tribes. It looked like an immense river of color, slowly surging forward.

That evening Jeremiah finally felt it was time to speak to Josh about a major worry he had. Everything was going well, but they had one insurmountable obstacle—the Bering Strait.

"Elder Brown, I know we've put this entire journey in the Lord's hands, but aren't you concerned about how we're going to get across the ocean? If it was winter, I could see the Lord freezing the water and creating an ice sheet for us to cross, but it's too warm for that to happen. I've also considered that we could build boats, but that could be time-consuming and doesn't seem practical."

Josh looked at him with a half-smile. "You're the scriptorian,

Jeremiah. You know that neither of those options are what the Lord has in mind for the group. Quote me the scripture that talks about what awaits us."

Jeremiah swallowed hard. "Well, it's part of the same verse in D&C 133 that we talked about earlier. It says, *"And an highway shall be cast up in the midst of the great deep."*

Josh nodded. "That's correct."

Jeremiah furrowed his brow. "But I don't understand where we're going to get the building materials. Even with all of these men here, getting enough materials to build a highway across the ocean is going to take us a long time, especially since we don't even have road-construction equipment."

Josh's grin widened. "Trust in the Lord, my friend. It actually won't take much time at all."

Two weeks later, the group was within a day of reaching the point along the Bering Strait that the scouts felt was most suitable for the people to camp. Most of the people in the group weren't geography buffs, so it never dawned on them that there was 55-mile waterway blocking their path to North America, but by tomorrow they would realize it, and if Josh didn't come through for them, there would be a million people stuck on a seashore with nowhere to go.

For the first time since the Ten Tribes began their journey, Josh was feeling really nervous. He still hadn't told anyone the details of how they would cross the Bering Strait, and he began to doubt his own abilities. As the butterflies started to build in his stomach, he slipped off into a grove of trees and knelt in prayer.

"Heavenly Father, I could use some reassurance right now. Please send John to me so I can talk to him about what I need to do."

He continued praying for several minutes, and then as he looked up, he saw his trusted friend standing in front of him.

"You're doing great," John told him. "I've been following the group and encouraging some of the stragglers to not give up. For the most part, everyone has been in good spirits."

Josh frowned slightly. "Things are going well, but I'm struggling with my self-confidence. I don't know if I can pull it off. Maybe you could stick around and help me out."

John suddenly got a concerned look on his face. "Not to put any pressure on you, but this is your assignment, not mine. Mathoni told me you did very well at moving the rocks to uncover the bus in Arizona."

"I know, but those were just boulders. This is a much bigger rock, if you know what I'm saying."

"It's the same principle," John said reassuringly. "The priesthood power that moved those rocks in Arizona is going to help you do the same thing tomorrow. Don't forget that this whole earth was created through priesthood power. Certainly you can move a small portion of it. It is the Lord's will, and he is counting on you. This miracle has many purposes, including strengthening the faith of the new members of the Church, and providing a unifying effect for all of these other people who have joined you along the way. Just as Moses led their ancestors across the Red Sea on dry ground, you'll soon do the same thing."

"Thank you for your confidence in me. I'm feeling better already." Then Josh shook his head and said, "I guess the biggest problem is that I keep asking myself, 'Why me?' I'm certainly not on the same level as Moses."

John smiled. "I believe every apostle and prophet has asked himself the same question. We know our own faults and weaknesses. I even asked the Lord once why I was chosen to write the Book of Revelation, and his answer was sufficient."

"What did he say?"

"He simply looked me in the eyes and said, 'Why *not* you?'"

Josh nodded solemnly. "Yes, that really does sum it up, doesn't it? Despite our limitations, the Lord trusts us to do his work."

John stepped forward and put his hand on Josh's shoulder. "I'm very pleased you're taking a humble approach to this. That's the sign of a true disciple. But now go forth and perform the task you've been given. Everything will work out as it should."

The next morning more than a million people were arriving at a two-mile stretch of seashore along the Bering Strait. At first most of the people thought they would just be walking north along the seashore, but many people were speculating that they were somehow going to cross the ocean. This news created some confusion among the people, and Jeremiah sensed it could develop into frustration and a sense of panic. He found Josh and said, "Whatever you're going to do, I wouldn't wait much longer."

Josh nodded and climbed onto a small rock outcropping that jutted slightly into the water. He faced the water and raised both arms, then in a loud voice he called out, "As an apostle of the Lord Jesus Christ, and by the power of the holy Melchizedek Priesthood that I hold, I command the earth that rests at the bottom of this sea to rise up out of the water and provide a passageway for the Children of Israel to cross over to the land of Zion. I do this in the sacred name of Jesus Christ, Amen."

Few people on the shore other than Jeremiah had actually heard Josh's words, and for a few seconds nothing happened. But Josh stood perfectly still, keeping his arms raised. His heart was beating wildly, watching for any indication that something was happening deep on the ocean floor.

Then a low rumble was heard, and Josh could faintly see what looked like a wave forming far out to sea. It had worked!

Suddenly the ground jolted sharply, and Josh hurried down from the outcropping while shouting, "Move away from the shore! A wave is coming! Get to higher ground!"

He and Jeremiah headed for a small knoll so they could get a better view of the sea, and by the time they reached the top of the knoll, the wave was less than a mile from shore. Beyond the wave it appeared that an island was rising from the water. All of the people along the shore were simultaneously moving inland and looking over their shoulders in wonder as the wave grew closer. A wide slab of rock was emerging from the sea, looking quite a bit like a massive highway, just as had been prophesied. The giant wave soon reached the shore and drenched several thousand people up to their waists, but it quickly dissipated without sweeping anyone away. Whatever discomfort the wave caused was quickly forgotten as the rocks that had formed the shoreline cracked loudly and then jutted several feet above sea level.

Everyone was quiet, astonished at what they saw. Josh gazed at what now lay before him. As far as he could see was an elevated layer of rock that was nearly a mile wide and fifteen feet above the sea.

The edges of the massive rock were quite jagged, evidence that it had literally been ripped from the sea bottom with tremendous force. However, the top of the rock was quite smooth. During the rock's upward journey, most of the sand and silt had been washed from its surface, providing a perfect highway for the Lost Tribes of Israel.

Jeremiah was smiling widely. "Elder Brown, you did it!"

Josh shook his head. "The Lord did it. I'm just glad no one drowned. Maybe we should've kept people away from the shore."

Jeremiah laughed, and suddenly they were joined by a third person.

"Well done, Elder Brown," John said, clasping his hand. "I just inspected the entire length of the bridge, and I would recommend you let it dry until tomorrow morning. It's a long way, and it will take about three days to cross even at a brisk pace, so make sure everyone has food and water before they begin. I'm sure the scientists in New Jerusalem have noted a major seismic event in this area, and the First Presidency will figure out what has happened, but I'm going to New Jerusalem today to report to them. The time has come to prepare a massive missionary effort to teach all of these people the gospel."

✤ ✤ ✤

The following day Josh sent the scout teams onto the rock. It was surreal to see them finally disappear in the distance. Two days later they returned to say they had gone far enough that they could see the bridge did indeed connect to Alaska. They also reported that it wasn't much different than walking on an uneven gravel road. Plus, the width of the land bridge would allow the whole group to move forward as a group, rather than having room for only a few thousand people at a time.

Josh was also pleased to see that the event did indeed touch the hearts of the people. They could clearly see the hand of God in it, especially as word spread that it had happened immediately after "Elder Brown" had said a special prayer. The people began referring to it simply as "The Miracle."

Three days after the bridge emerged, the people were prepared with plenty of food and water, and they were very anxious to get started. Josh held a meeting with all of the village leaders, explaining that a safe crossing was the objective, rather than getting across first.

To emphasize the point, Josh told them, "Jeremiah will lead the way, but I will be the last person across. I want everyone to make it safely. All I ask is that you don't start the next leg of the journey without me!"

Later that morning, Josh gave Jeremiah a quick embrace, and then stood on the shore as the members of Jeremiah's ward stepped onto the bridge. Many of them spotted him and called out, "See you soon, Elder Brown! We love you!"

Josh's eyes filled with tears as he realized how close he felt to these people. As Jeremiah's group moved forward and other groups followed them, Josh walked again to the top of the nearby knoll. It was an emotional moment to watch the Lost Tribes of Israel depart from the continent where they had long been hidden and excitedly walk toward their new home in Zion. The younger people all had an extra bounce in their step, but the older ones did too.

Josh suddenly sensed several other people standing on the knoll with him. He couldn't see them, but they were as tangible as he was. He knew that many ancient prophets had seen this day in vision, and he supposed that the Lord had allowed them to now witness it firsthand.

Josh soon felt a powerful surge of energy pass through him, as if he was receiving a giant group hug. His entire body felt like it was filled with a spiritual flame, and for a few seconds he could actually hear these fellow servants thanking him for his service. His testimony of the Spirit World was already unshakable, but now that testimony had moved from mere faith to pure knowledge.

Josh could only bow his head and say, "Thank thee, Heavenly Father, for granting me this experience."

# CHAPTER 20

—⚬—

Back in New Jerusalem, the prophet sat in his office pondering the events that were about to take place. He had met with John the Revelator the previous evening, and since that time he had felt a weight upon him that he needed to speak to the Saints. The time had come for them to take another step forward in becoming a Zion people.

John had told him that Elder Brown was leading more than a million members of the Ten Tribes toward the city. The Saints had easily handled new groups arriving in the city, but never on this scale. John also informed him that only about a thousand of these people were members of the Church—and brand new ones at that. This fact would add to the challenge of assimilating the new arrivals into Zion, although it sounded like these people had essentially been living the Law of Consecration for many years in their small villages.

The prophet called the other members of the First Presidency into his office and shared John's report with them. They agreed that the Saints needed to know about these developments, and so the prophet asked his secretary to come into his office. "We need to announce that I'll address the Saints in New Jerusalem this afternoon at four o'clock," he told her. "It will be broadcast to all of the stake centers throughout the city. If at all possible, every Saint should be in attendance."

A few hours later the prophet stood at a podium on the edge of the temple plaza. He looked out over the vast audience that had assembled there, and he knew that hundreds of thousands of Saints were also congregated in their meetinghouses across the city.

"What a marvelous sight it is to see such a large gathering," the prophet began. "Thank you for taking time out of your day to hear this message. I know we have General Conference coming up soon in October, but I've received wonderful news that I'm pleased to share with you today."

He then opened a set of scriptures and said, "Let me first introduce the topic by reading a verse that many of you memorized as children. It's the Tenth Article of Faith, and it says, '*We believe in the literal gathering of Israel and in the restoration of the Ten Tribes; that Zion (the New Jerusalem) will be built upon the American continent; that Christ will reign personally upon the earth; and, that the earth will be renewed and receive its paradisiacal glory.*'

"Joseph Smith wrote the Articles of Faith in 1842, and they were mainly written to explain our beliefs to non-members . The first nine Articles of Faith are quite basic and straight-forward. Then comes this one that mentions the Ten Tribes, New Jerusalem, the Second Coming, and the Millennium. To the Saints of 1842, it must have exceeded their biggest dreams. I admit that as a young man in the 1960s that verse sounded like science fiction even to me."

Many people in the audience chuckled, because they could relate to what the prophet was saying.

"However, we've finally reached the point in time when these events are taking place," the prophet continued. "Several weeks ago I authorized Elder Joshua Brown of the Quorum of the Twelve to travel to Siberia, and I have received the wonderful news that he is now leading members of the Ten Tribes to join us here in New Jerusalem. They are more than a million strong, and they should arrive within a month."

The prophet's announcement sent a buzz of excitement through the audience. The Saints knew that this was a major event that needed to take place before the Second Coming.

The prophet cleared his throat and continued, "The curious thing about the tribes is that they have only recently come to understand their true identity as descendants of the Israelites, and only about a thousand of them are brand-new members of the Church. In other words, these people don't have a strong understanding of the gospel. However, I've heard from a good source that they're willing to follow the Savior and become members of his Church. For that reason I am now calling all single young men between the ages of 19 and 24 to serve as missionaries to this great multitude. Unlike our missionaries of the past, you don't have to go find your golden converts, they're coming to you! Single women over the age of 21 who desire to be missionaries may also serve."

The prophet smiled. "I know this is somewhat of a relief to many of you who received patriarchal blessings that indicated you would serve a mission. I know that some of you wondered if those patriarchs had been wrong and whether the chance to serve a mission would ever come. But now you have a unique opportunity to teach and help convert thousands of people."

He paused and looked out across the audience, catching the eyes of several excited young men sitting as a group. He nodded toward them, and one of them pumped his fist in the air and cried out, "Woo hoo!" The audience members around him gave a collective laugh, and the prophet laughed as well.

"Young man, I certainly agree with your assessment of the situation," the prophet said. "It's going to be very exciting. Of course, it's vital that you are properly trained, and so each of you will be assigned to a Missionary Training Center for the next few weeks where former mission presidents and MTC instructors will help you be prepared to share the gospel when the Ten Tribes arrive. Please contact your bishop immediately to notify him that you plan on serving, and then you'll receive your assignment."

The prophet shuffled his papers on the podium, then said, "Let me switch gears for a moment. Behind me you see this magnificent temple. The exterior has been completed, and we are very close to finishing the work on the interior. After consulting with the construction managers this past week, we have determined that the temple will be ready for dedication by mid-September. In accordance, I have determined that the temple's first dedicatory session will be held on September 22. That date has significance in Church history as the date that Joseph Smith received the gold plates from the angel Moroni in 1827. Now it will also be remembered as the day that the New Jerusalem Temple was dedicated to the Lord. In my mind, this temple's shining gold beams are symbolic of those golden plates. The plates themselves were never allowed to be used for material gain, and neither will the gold that adorns this temple. Both the plates and the beams draw our eyes heavenward in remembrance of our eternal goals.

"As you know, new temples are being built from this Center Point five miles apart in every direction. Hopefully someday we'll be able to send a satellite into space to photograph it, but from the heavens I envision our city will look like a miniature galaxy, with this main temple as the blazing center with smaller points of light surrounding it in a precise pattern, providing a reminder of our heavenly home."

The prophet suddenly became emotional, hardly able to speak. Finally he said, "The veil is growing thinner. A few days ago I was awakened by an angel who beckoned me to follow him. He led me into the Spirit World. I told the angel I wasn't ready to die, and he simply smiled and said I was only visiting.

"He then took me to a gleaming white city that seemed like a university campus. We entered an enormous library where thousands of men and women in white robes were transcribing written records and typing them into computers. This seemed curious to me, because it seemed like an earthly task, similar to the Family History indexing program we have. The angel told me, 'These people are transcribing the spiritual versions of records that were once written on earth but were destroyed through the centuries. They are compiling the records into family groups and pedigrees so that the work can be done for the righteous souls who are still waiting in Spirit Prison.'

"The angel took me beside one of the women who was compiling a family group sheet. It looked similar to the ones we use here on earth. She handed me a record for a family that had lived on earth when the Nephite civilization began to crumble. I noticed the father was named Lamah, and he had been born in 356 A.D. in the city of Zarahemla. The record indicated he had been baptized into the Church of Jesus Christ in 364 A.D. as an eight-year-old.

"The angel told me, 'Lamah was a great man, but due to his earthly circumstances he never was able to take his family to the temple, because of the apostasy that had taken place. He was one of the prophet Mormon's captains in the final battle against the Lamanites, and he was killed by them, along with his wife and three children. They have all been waiting for many centuries to be sealed as a family.'

"As I looked at the group sheet, I told the angel I wanted to take it back with me and take care of their sealing immediately. The angel smiled again and said, 'Soon enough. You must return and prepare the Saints to have the Spirit in greater measure. Then the information will be made available to them.'

"Then my mind was opened on how this would happen. I saw angels visiting our temples carrying folders filled with family history information. They will ask us to transcribe the information into our earthly computers and prepare the names for temple work. It will eliminate any guesswork. The angels will know who is ready to receive the ordinances of the gospel, and the work will progress rapidly. With the arrival of the Ten Tribes, I know that their ancestors will also be eager for their temple work to be completed. I expect our temples to be operating six days a week, 24 hours a day as we move into this new phase of temple work.

"Then to emphasize his point, the angel guided me out of the building and we soared through the sky at a rapid speed. We crossed a great gulf of water and then gazed across a spacious land filled with seemingly millions of people. The angel said, 'This is the edge of Spirit Prison. It extends far beyond the horizon, but all of these people are waiting to become members of the Church and enter Paradise. It is up to the Saints in Zion to assist them by performing their temple ordinances.'

"The angel then returned me to my body and I awoke feeling anxious to step up our pace here in Zion. We need missionaries, we need to complete additional temples, and we need to prepare homes for the Ten Tribes. As I prayed about where in Zion the new arrivals should live, I felt prompted that we should refurbish several cities to the south of us in the next few weeks. Construction crews will be organized, and it is my greatest desire that we can give them the kind of welcome that has been prophesied."

The prophet opened his scriptures once again and read concerning the Ten Tribes from D&C 133:32-33: "*And there they shall fall down and be crowned with glory, even in Zion, by the hands of the servants of the Lord, even the children of Ephraim. And they shall be filled with songs of everlasting joy.*"

He gazed intently at the audience for several seconds, and then said, "That is our commission, my brothers and sisters. I know we will succeed with the Lord's help. I now send you forth with my prophetic blessing that each of us will fulfill our assignments during this historic time."

# CHAPTER 21

The Norths and Daltons gathered together in Emma and Tad's yard following the prophet's message, and they discussed the many wonderful things he had mentioned in his talk.

Becky Dalton in particular was excited about his description of what was happening in the Spirit World. This had always been an interest of hers since the death of her parents a few years earlier. She felt they were teaching the gospel to their ancestors, and the prophet's words gave her hope that additional breakthroughs would come soon.

Becky and Phyllis had already bonded over family history work. As a convert to the Church, Phyllis was eager to work on her own family history and get her relatives' names processed for the temple, and Becky had helped her already locate hundreds of her ancestors through the U.S. Census records.

Of course, the prophet's call for missionaries had caught David's attention, and he was eager to serve, even though it would put his budding relationship with Phyllis on hold. She was still only 20 and wouldn't be able to serve as a full-time missionary.

That evening the pair took a walk through the nearby park, trying to sort out their emotions. David expected to be gone at least several weeks, if not months. He and Phyllis had certainly become good friends and having classes together at BYU-Zion meant they had spent a lot of time working on homework. They had reached the point that his family now teased him about his "girlfriend." He hadn't argued with them, but he hadn't even kissed her yet.

The biggest obstacle in his mind was that he wasn't sure of her true feelings for him. Did she really like him, or was he just a nice safety blanket as she adjusted to all the changes in her life?

They took a seat on a bench. "I'm really eager to serve a mission, but I'm going to miss you," David said, looking in her eyes. "You've become my best friend."

Phyllis smiled. "I feel the same way about you. I don't know if I can get through my classes without you there to help me."

She then paused and looked at the ground. "David, do you find me . . . attractive?"

David kind of jerked back, and Phyllis took it the wrong way. "I'm sorry, I shouldn't have—"

"I sure do," David said, cutting her off. "In fact, I think you're beautiful."

Phyllis' cheeks brightened. "Really? I . . . uh, really?"

David took her hands in his. "That's why I wanted to talk to you tonight. We've only known each other a couple of months, but I really like you, and my only fear about going on a mission is that while I'm gone you'll meet one of those actual returned missionaries and get swept off your feet."

Phyllis laughed. "That's not going to happen. I've already got my eye on someone."

David frowned. "I knew it. Is it that guy Bart in our Biology class? I've seen how he looks at you and I—"

She suddenly moved closer and planted a kiss firmly on his lips. As he sat there stunned, she backed away and said, "No, you goofball. It's you."

David was feeling so many emotions that he could hardly talk. He suspected this was what being in love felt like. Finally he sputtered, "That's good. That's what I was hoping."

She laughed again. "Don't worry, I'm not going anywhere. I live with your grandparents, for heaven's sake. Since they're going to suspend our classes because of all of the missionaries leaving, Becky and I are going to really focus on my family history while you're away. We'll see how it goes from there when you get back, but I don't foresee any changes."

David simply nodded, then smiled briefly before giving her a kiss in return.

David was assigned to a Missionary Training Center a few days later that was nearly two hundred miles away from his home on the city's southern border. Since the plan was to locate the Ten Tribes in that region, the Church leaders felt it would work best to have the missionaries already there. Like previous missionaries, David had one P-Day each week, and he was able to send the family an e-mail that day. Everyone enjoyed hearing how he was progressing.

The missionaries had been told that most of the members of the Ten Tribes spoke a little bit of English, so they were learning the missionary discussions in that language since they didn't have any materials prepared in the tribes' various dialects. David said the Church leaders were confident they would be able to rely on the gift of tongues if needed. He said they were learning the discussions from a newly updated version of *Preach My Gospel* and he thanked his parents for using that book as the basis for their Family Home Evening lessons for many years. He wrote, "You'll be happy to know that while I was sitting in a stupor on the couch each Monday night, some of it actually sank in!"

Besides studying intensely in the MTC, David and his fellow missionaries also spent two days a week helping rebuild the abandoned cities for the tribes, and the mix of work and study had the missionaries fired up and in good spirits. David couldn't wait for the "golden contacts" to arrive.

At last the day of the temple dedication arrived, and a celebration of epic proportions was planned.

One tradition concerning temples that had disappeared after the establishment of New Jerusalem was the "temple open house." With new temples being built five miles apart, the First Presidency realized that getting the temples operational as soon as possible was the most important thing to do. They reasoned that nearly all adults in New Jerusalem held temple recommends and could attend temple sessions, and every young person over the age of twelve was scheduled to participate in baptisms for the dead at their closest temple at least once a month.

However, demand for tickets to the temple dedication of the New Jerusalem Temple were high, and only a few thousand would be able to attend in person. Emma was thrilled to discover that those who had labored on the temple itself were given preference, and since Tad was one of a few dozen men who had worked continuously on the temple from the day when the first brick was laid, he was given two seats inside the temple dome where the dedication would take place.

On the morning of the dedication, Tad and Emma eagerly walked hand in hand along with thousands of other Saints toward the temple, all dressed in white. They entered the temple's central dome, and Emma was still amazed to see there weren't any support beams on the inside of it—the arched design supported all the weight. The 24 smaller temple structures were connected at ground level by glass-enclosed walkways, but there were also elevated walkways that linked the terraced flower gardens that were growing atop each of the buildings.

These gardens reminded Emma of the meadow and gardens that were atop the Conference Center in Salt Lake City. As magnificent as the Conference Center was, she realized it had been merely a practice run for the immense, awe-inspiring structure that towered above her.

The elevated walkways provided a unifying effect and tied the 24 buildings together, making the temple look like a great crown from a distance. The Saints felt such symbolism was perfect for the home of the "King of Kings." Indeed, this temple lived up to being the House of the Lord.

Emma also thought of how each of those smaller buildings were symbolic of tent stakes, helping to strengthen and support a large tent, just as the stakes of the Church supported the Church itself. She smiled to think that those 24 buildings were considered small, since they were each the size of the Provo Temple. Each building had a specific purpose related to the temple ordinances, but she knew there was a specific one where the First Presidency and Twelve Apostles would meet together often.

The Church leaders would continue to have their individual offices in the nearby Church Administration Building, but much like the Salt Lake Temple had been for previous Church administrations, this temple would now be the spiritual center for the First Presidency and the Twelve Apostles as they sought inspiration in handling their responsibilities.

The couple made their way to their seats, and they discovered they would be sitting directly underneath the central spire. They paused to look straight up, but it was so high that it made Emma feel dizzy.

The dedication ceremony soon began. The Mormon Tabernacle Choir—still intact and larger than ever— performed two beautiful numbers, and the spirit in the temple was nearly overpowering. Emma hadn't ever felt such sheer joy. It was as if the earthly cares of the world had been stripped away, and she was being allowed to feel how it would someday feel in the Celestial Kingdom.

She noticed that everyone around her seemed to be experiencing the same sensations. Tad looked at her with tears in his eyes and whispered, "I've never felt so happy."

The prophet then stood at the pulpit and commented on the powerful spirit that was there. "This morning I have felt surrounded by many of my fellow apostles who have passed on to the other side of the veil," he said. "They are here with us and I can sense their excitement and happiness that this momentous day has finally come."

Emma suddenly spotted men and women in white robes walking along the temple's outside walkways, although they clearly weren't mortal, since many of them were hovering several feet above the ground to get a better view of the main pulpit. The prophet waved to them, and they waved back.

Then an "Aaaahh" went up from the congregation as several empty seats on the stand behind the prophet were suddenly filled by men in white suits. Emma could hardly contain her emotions as she recognized the previous presidents of the Church of Jesus Christ of Latter-day Saints sitting in order. They all looked so young and vibrant, although Emma smiled to see that they retained their unique physical characteristics. President Gordon B. Hinckley still looked small when sitting next to President Thomas S. Monson. It was a curious scene that seemed so natural if one didn't stop to ponder how amazing it was.

The prophet turned to his predecessors and welcomed them. "You're all looking so good. I'm so glad you are here."

The prophet gave some introductory remarks about the rise of Zion in the latter days. He then read the temple dedicatory prayer, emphasizing the sacredness of the area where the temple now stood, from the time of Adam and Eve to the present day. At the conclusion of the prayer, he led the congregation in the traditional "Hosanna Shout." As they concluded, the glass panels of the dome began to vibrate.

Everyone looked around in wonderment. A pillar of light was descending on the temple. It engulfed the outside buildings, and then came inside the temple dome itself, energizing and saturating everyone and everything inside. Emma held her arms out in front of her, and they glowed. She looked at Tad's face, and it was also glowing. Even their clothes seemed to radiate brighter than before.

The Tabernacle Choir began singing "The Spirit of God Like a Fire is Burning" and Emma now comprehended the meaning of the song on an entirely new level. She was indeed burning with the Spirit of God, but it wasn't painful. Instead, it was a feeling she hoped to hold onto throughout eternity.

As the choir concluded the song, a voice was faintly heard. Everyone went silent, and the voice came again, "*I am Jesus Christ.*

*I accept this house as my own, and I accept this people as my own.*"

No one in the temple could hardly speak, because their hearts were too full, but Emma and Tad embraced, and Tad said a prayer of thanks in his heart for the power of repentance and the Savior's atoning sacrifice. He shuddered to think of how his previous errors and foolishness had nearly cost him his beautiful wife and children, as well as the opportunity to live in Zion.

"I love you," he whispered in Emma's ear, never wanting to let her go.

As the dedication was taking place, the Ten Tribes were still several miles away, walking across a grassy plain on the outskirts of Zion's northern farms and agricultural areas. If all went well, they would reach New Jerusalem's outer communities within the next couple of days.

Jeremiah watched his son Peter scamper around in the lush prairie grass on the edge of the road. Peter usually rode in one of the wagons they had built, so it paid off to let him get out his wiggles early in the day.

Suddenly an intense light pierced the southern sky. The light then shot to the ground, appearing to be a glowing ball of fire on the horizon.

Jeremiah stopped in his tracks. The light was almost too bright to look at directly. He turned his gaze toward his son and saw Peter crawling through the grass toward him while keeping a steady gaze on the ball of light.

"What is it, Papa?" the boy asked.

"I think it's from Heavenly Father," his father responded. "Let's go talk with Elder Brown."

Jeremiah gently scooped Peter off the grass and put him on his shoulders. As they rejoined their group, everyone was gazing at the astounding sight in the distance.

Jeremiah found Elder Brown and asked, "Do you think a nuclear bomb has gone off?"

Elder Brown smiled. "No, it's not a bomb. I believe a marvelous event is taking place. The prophet wanted to have the temple completed and operational by the time our group arrived, and in our recent meetings with the First Presidency he often talked about wanting to dedicate the temple on September 22, which is today. It appears the dedication is underway, and the Lord has blessed the Saints with a powerful outpouring of his love for us."

Word quickly spread through the traveling groups about what Josh had said, and within a few minutes all of the Ten Tribes had stopped traveling and were spread out across the grassy plain to gaze upon the tremendous light to the south. Everyone was mesmerized by it. The light remained bright for more than an hour, then it eventually began to ebb away.

The tribes felt energized by the experience. It had been a long journey, but now the end was in sight, and soon they were all marching forward with a renewed vigor, heading toward their new home.

# CHAPTER 22

It had been two days since the pillar of light had engulfed the temple. Jeremiah still felt invigorated by what he had witnessed, even from such a distance. That morning he had helped lead the Ten Tribes into the northern suburbs of New Jerusalem, where the Saints had greeted them with open arms and treated them like family. As they neared the city center, he had noticed the city's elegant architecture, attractive homes, and luxurious flowerbeds. Jeremiah felt like the city had been scrubbed clean just for their arrival.

"I think we're going to like it here," Jeremiah told his wife Tasha as they walked up the road.

She nodded enthusiastically. "Yes, everything is so beautiful."

Elder Brown had been in contact with the prophet, who told him to lead the tribes straight to the temple site. The temple was so tall that it was now easily in view, and Jeremiah was nearly overwhelmed by its size and grandeur. He thought back on the trials and struggles they had faced during the three months it had taken them to reach Zion, but he knew they had been greatly blessed. There had hardly been any illnesses among the group. There had been a few deaths among some of the older people, and they had been buried along the way, but injuries and accidents had been rare.

Much like when the Ute tribe had brought the sacred gold into the city, the citizens of Zion lined up along streets to greet the new arrivals. However, this greeting was on a much more massive scale than before. Everyone wanted to get a glimpse of the Ten Tribes.

After all, they had been lost for so long! To the disappointment of some, other than differing styles of clothing, the tribes looked quite a bit like they did.

At last the group began arriving at the temple plaza, and as they gathered they began singing a long-cherished song that focused on joy and happiness. The song had been handed down through their families for generations and had been translated into English in recent years. The song seemed perfectly fitting for this moment, and the surrounding crowd listened attentively, struck by the song's beauty.

Soon the prophet emerged, standing on a raised tower in the center of the plaza so everyone could see him. There were also video screens and loudspeakers spread across the plaza to transmit the prophet's message.

He then welcomed them to Zion and then said, "Thank you for that wonderful song. We have been told that the Ten Tribes would bring their treasures with them, and that song certainly qualifies as one of them."

The crowd clapped enthusiastically in agreement. The prophet continued, "What a week it has been. First we had a tremendous outpouring of the Spirit at the dedication of the New Jerusalem Temple, and now we are greatly honored to be in the presence of the Ten Tribes. The scriptures have long prophesied of when the Ten Tribes would return once again from the north countries and be united with the other children of the House of Israel, the descendants of Abraham, Isaac, and Jacob. Some people have said you were lost, but that's not really true, is it? The Lord knew where you were, and now the wonderful promises of the Lord will be set in motion."

The prophet explained that the plan was to house the tribes at meetinghouses throughout the city over the next few days to evaluate their needs and record their personal and family information. He also explained that homes had been prepared for them in the southern part of the city, and the tribe members were overjoyed to hear that news. There was a great feeling of unity in the city as the citizens of Zion led families to the meetinghouses and helped them begin to settle in.

After the prophet came down from the tower, Josh introduced Jeremiah to the First Presidency. Jeremiah instinctively bowed before them.

"Please stand up," the prophet said with a smile, touching Jeremiah's shoulder. "In many ways, I feel I should be the one bowing before you."

Jeremiah grinned sheepishly as he stood. "I'm sorry. I've just waited so long to meet the prophet of the Lord. It's a great honor to be here."

Elder Brown then motioned to a wooden cart that Jeremiah had kept near his side during the entire journey. "President, we have a very important delivery to make to you."

Jeremiah had momentarily forgotten about the cart, but he quickly pulled it closer. "That's right. These are for you."

Jeremiah opened the lid of the cart and removed a blanket that covered the three sets of three ancient metal plates.

Josh explained, "Jeremiah's family members have been the keepers of the records of their people for many centuries. We fully expect that these plates contain the Savior's visit to the Ten Tribes that the Lord spoke of in the Book of Mormon."

Jeremiah removed one set of plates and carefully handed it to the prophet. "I believe this is the oldest set," he said. "No one among our people can read the inscriptions, but Elder Brown has told me how you have already translated plates that were written by the Nephite historians, so I'm hopeful that you can do the same with these records. I know that my people are already curious and interested in becoming members of the Church, but if they can read the words and testimonies of their ancestors, they'll be even more receptive to the gospel message."

"I agree completely," the prophet said. "I'll start the translation this evening."

Josh then pulled out a fist-sized rock from his pocket and handed it to the prophet. "I also brought this for you. I thought you'd like to see it. This is a part of the Siberian land bridge that we crossed. I brought it with me, thinking it would make a nice addition to our newly reopened Church History Museum."

The prophet studied the rock. "I'm glad you brought this back. What a marvelous piece of history."

As soon as he could possibly break away, Josh rushed to find Kim and the twins. The journey back had taken much too long. As they embraced and held each other close, he wished he could have taken Kim and the kids with him. However, he realized that everything had worked out as it was supposed to. He had been able to fully concentrate on his duties as an apostle, while his wife and children had been able to enjoy the comforts of Zion. But Josh didn't want to be away from his family for that long ever again.

The next two weeks were a whirlwind of excitement and constant hustle and bustle as the members of the Ten Tribes made their way on buses to their new homes. Not every house was quite up to the modern standards yet that was expected in Zion—most didn't have new carpet or a computer—but the homes all had indoor plumbing and electricity, and the new arrivals thought everything was wonderful. Any other conveniences could be added later.

Much like previous arrivals, the members of the Ten Tribes formed neighborhoods with their friends and neighbors they had known in Siberia. However, the members of Jeremiah's Siberian ward lived in a neighborhood in the center of the new settlements, Jeremiah had specifically requested for that arrangement so he and the other Siberian priesthood holders could spread out from that location and teach the gospel, working with the thousands of missionaries who were already in the area.

David North was right in the midst of it all. The missionaries didn't make any attempts to preach the gospel yet. He and his companion had simply been assigned to meet the needs of the families on a certain block and make sure they were settled in. It was a little mind-boggling to watch thousands of abandoned houses suddenly be filled with thousands of energetic families.

David felt particularly close to the Khudi family, a young couple on that block with three little children. They had lived deep in the forests of Siberia their entire lives, but they told David of a premonition they'd both received about a year earlier that they would be moving a great distance. They had discussed it, but there hadn't been any reason to believe it would happen.

Then the visitor named John came to their village and spoke about a group that would pass by on their way to a heavenly city. The couple had smiled at each other when they heard him speak, knowing they were already mentally prepared to make the journey.

David knew the Lord had paved the way for that family to be in Zion, and he felt it was only a matter of time before the Khudis would be members of the Church.

✤ ✤ ✤

As the first weekend in October approached, the Ten Tribes were mostly settled into their new homes, and the First Presidency announced that General Conference would move forward as scheduled.

The prophet's opening address on Saturday morning summarized the amazing developments of the past few weeks, and he welcomed once again the Ten Tribes, knowing that most of them were watching in school auditoriums near their homes, since meetinghouses hadn't yet been constructed in that area.

"One of the great aspects of the return of the Ten Tribes, is that one of their people, Bishop Jeremiah Yakovlevna, brought with him the ancient records of their people," the prophet said. "Bishop Yakovlevna was gracious enough to allow me to translate them into English, and fortunately the translation is progressing well. I was pleased to discover that much like Mormon had been inspired to compile an abridgement of the Nephite history, a similar prophet had done so concerning the early years of the Ten Tribes."

The prophet continued, "As you know, during his visit among

the ancient inhabitants of this continent, the Savior said in Third Nephi 17:4, '*But now I go unto the Father, and also to show myself unto the lost tribes of Israel, for they are not lost unto the Father, for he knoweth whither he hath taken them.*' I am delighted to tell you that the Savior's visit is included in this record, and you'll all be fascinated as you read it. The Savior shared with them many profound yet simple gospel teachings that provide another witness of the truthfulness of the gospel. The record expounds on doctrines that were only briefly mentioned in the Book of Mormon.

"It's my belief that the Savior knew this record would come forth at this time when we as Saints are able to better appreciate these so-called mysteries of the kingdom, many of which have not been fully revealed until now. I know that each of us will be uplifted and edified as we read this record. It is fascinating and will increase your gospel knowledge and faith in the Lord."

The prophet smiled. "Many of you have been asking when the translation will be complete. I have translated the first of the three records, and it is the one that includes the Savior's visit among them. Right now we are hurriedly getting the book typeset so everyone can read it. We expect to have the online version ready by the end of next week. I testify that this record is approved by the Lord and can stand alongside the other canonized books of scripture. I'm sure that in the future we'll divide it up into verses and cross-reference it with the other scriptures, but first I ask you to just read it and appreciate it for the wonderful story that it is."

By the end of the following week, everyone was devouring *The Record of the Ten Tribes*. The truths the book contained took the Saints to new heights of gospel understanding, and it helped them take another step closer to becoming a Zion people.

That same week the prophet asked Mark Dalton to meet with him. Mark was surprised and couldn't think of a reason why the prophet would want to see him. He knew the prophet had been appreciative of his service with the Ute tribe in bringing the sacred gold to New Jerusalem, but now he was ready to just settle down and serve in his community temple for a few hours each day.

As Mark entered the prophet's office, the prophet stood and shook his hand warmly. "Thank you for coming," the prophet said. "I hope you've enjoyed the events of the past few weeks."

Mark nodded, "It's been wonderful. It is amazing how Zion is expanding so rapidly, yet everything is still so orderly and peaceful."

"I agree," the prophet said. "However, I'm afraid you can't quite slip into full-time temple service yet."

"What do you mean?"

"There's still work to be done outside of Zion. The Lord has an errand for you to complete. He would like you to help reclaim Salt Lake City from Sherem and his followers. Now that New Jerusalem is firmly established, the time has come to repopulate the Wasatch Front with Saints and have the temples fully operational again."

"I agree that Salt Lake needs to be reclaimed, but why me? I'm getting to be an old man," Mark said. "Besides, I've never led an army before."

The prophet shook his head. " I never said you'd be leading an army. The Lord simply indicated that you are the one who should be called to regain the city."

Mark shrugged. "You know I'll do anything you ask of me, but where do I even start?"

The prophet paused for a moment. "The Lord mentioned that you should take with you a man named Jonas Ferguson. Do you know him?"

"A little bit," Mark said. "He's a friend of my son-in-law Tad. But I can't imagine how he could help."

"Neither do I, but that's the Lord's will," the prophet said. "I propose that you and Tad travel with Jonas to the Provo Temple. When you arrive, opportunities will open up to you. I know we could send in an army and get into a bloody battle with Sherem's men, but many lives would be lost on both sides, and I don't feel that is the will of the Lord. Sherem certainly has the homefield advantage, but I think that with some careful planning, he can be outwitted."

Mark felt a bit overwhelmed, but he also felt strangely confident. "Very well," he said. "I'll contact Jonas and Tad, and we'll be on our way to Provo."

# CHAPTER 23

———— ✦ ————

Mark, Tad and Jonas had departed for Provo within two days of Mark's meeting with the prophet. Mark had become considerably more excited about the assignment when he met with Jonas and discovered he had once been part of Sherem's inner circle.

To begin their assignment, each man had driven a solar-powered truck filled with canned food to Utah. The food was meant for the missionary guards and their families who were living at the Provo Temple. They arrived at the temple without any difficulties along the way, and the families there were thrilled to see them.

As Tad helped unload the food from one of the trucks, he suddenly felt a hand on his shoulder. "Hey, old friend," a soft voice said.

Tad turned to see Angie Thomason, one of Emma's close friends when she was younger. He was delighted to see her.

"Angie! You're alive! Emma and I have talked about you a lot. She even searched all of the databases in New Jerusalem, but she never could find you."

Angie smiled sadly. "We never did make it to Zion. My husband Kyle developed pancreatic cancer while we were living at the Heber Valley Camp, and since he was too weak to travel, we stayed behind when the group left for Zion. Kyle held on for several more weeks, but he finally succumbed to the cancer. So my son Tom and I came here to the temple rather than try to travel to Zion alone. Besides, we had been informed that my father was serving as a guard here."

"I'm sorry about Kyle," Tad said. "He was a great man."

Tad looked around for Angie's son, who he remembered as a husky youngster with fiery red hair who Emma had nicknamed Mighty Tom.

"So Tom is living here with you?" Tad asked.

"Yep, that's him over by the truck," she said, pointing to a well-built young man who was unloading 50-pound sacks of flour with ease. Tad was stunned to see how strong Tom had gotten. He walked over and introduced himself. Tom grabbed his hand and smiled. "Hey, I remember you. You're the Tadinator!"

Tad shook his head. "I haven't been called that for a long time, Mighty Tom."

Tom smiled. "I haven't been called that in years, either."

"Man, you've really filled out," Tad said, pointing at Tom's bulging biceps. "Too bad BYU's football team doesn't exist anymore. You would've made a great linebacker."

When the trucks were unloaded, Angie took Tad aside and peppered him with questions about how his family was doing. "I really miss Emma being around," Angie told him. "Without her friendship, who knows how Tom and I would have turned out?"

Tad knew that Angie had been one of Emma's good friends during high school, but they had drifted apart after graduation. Angie had made some poor choices, eventually getting pregnant as a teenager and giving birth to Tom. She was raising Tom as a single mother in Springville when Emma had a powerful spiritual experience that had prompted her to reconnect with Angie.

At first, Angie had been wary about Emma's sudden interest in her and her son, but they soon became close friends once again. Emma was thrilled when Angie had married Kyle, a returned missionary who had overlooked Angie's teenage troubles, and they had been active in the Church ever since.

Over the years, Emma had fretted over Mighty Tom almost as much as her own children. Tad understood her worries, because Tom had a wild side that sometimes surfaced in the wrong circumstances. He did get in trouble during junior high, becoming a bit of a bully, but whenever Angie would call Emma in despair about Tom's antics, Emma would reassure her it would be all right. Then she would hang up the phone and tell Tad, "Guess who you're taking to the Conquest game tonight?"

So Tad took Mighty Tom to a few Gladiatorzz games, and he was grateful he'd been able to say just the right things during those times to get Tom back on the right track. So other than a few minor skirmishes with the law, Tom had turned out pretty well, and Tad was pleased to see he had turned into a righteous young man.

As Angie and Tad continued talking, Tom came up to them. "Mom, I was wondering if Tad could give me a ride down to the Bean Museum in his truck. I need to feed the animals."

Angie shrugged and looked at Tad. "Would that be all right with you?"

"I suppose," Tad said. "I know Mark Dalton wants to have a meeting later tonight, but that should work out."

Tad checked with Mark, and he said it would be fine. The pair drove down the hill to the museum that was just east of the Marriott Center on the BYU campus. Along the way, they saw a column of smoke rising from Lincoln Point across Utah Lake.

"What's going on over there?" Tad asked. "I didn't notice the smoke as we were coming into the valley."

Tom shook his head. "There's a group of renegade kids over there who think they're going to conquer us someday. They sometimes come over to Provo, and we keep an eye on them in case they decide to attack the temple for our food."

"Is it a large group?" Tad asked.

"There's at least a couple hundred of them, but they aren't really organized," Tom said. "If they had a real leader who could rally them together, then we'd have to worry."

Soon Tad and Tom were pulling into the crumbling parking lot of the Bean Museum. "So you've got some pets here?" Tad asked as they got out of the truck and entered the building. "That's nice that you can have a hobby."

"Yeah, I've pretty much had the museum to myself for a while now," Tom said. "It's been fun."

"What kind of pets do you have here?"

"Actually, I have three dogs upstairs, a few parakeets, some chipmunks, and even a turtle. But I keep my favorite pet in the basement."

"What is it? Something exotic?" Tad asked.

"You could say that," Tom said.

They went down into the basement, where Tom went to an ice box and pulled out a large slab of meat.

"What's that?" Tad asked.

"Deer meat. During the winter we stock up at the temple, and I bring the less desirable pieces here for Sammy."

Just then Tom opened a door and a thick, 25-foot-long snake slithered out the door toward them.

"H-h-holy—" Tad shouted as he sprinted partway up the stairs.

Tom laughed loudly as the snake ignored Tad and began working on the slab of deer meat. "Sammy is as playful as a puppy," he said. "Come rub his head."

Tad stayed put near the top of the stairway, peering through the railing. "I'm fine right here," he said nervously. "That thing is your pet? That's just freaky."

"Hey, be nice," Tom said. "Sammy has never given me any trouble at all."

"Does your mom know about him?" Tad asked.

Tom shrugged nonchalantly. "She doesn't know he's so big. I haven't bothered telling her that he's grown wildly over the past year. I'd like to keep it that way."

Tad nodded. "My lips are sealed."

Tom soon put Sammy back in his room, and they returned to the temple, although Tad's legs still felt like jelly from the fright Sammy had put into him.

✤ ✤ ✤

That evening Tad, Jonas, and Mark got together to discuss their plans. Mark had asked each of them to ponder ways Sherem could be defeated as they drove to Utah, and now they were going to put their ideas together and see what they had come up with.

The temple workers had told them that Sherem still had guards posted in a shack at the Point of the Mountain, but they all agreed that after more than a year without any sign of intruders coming to the Salt Lake Valley, the guards had likely been lulled into a false sense of security.

"I don't think the members of Sherem's so-called army will pose much resistance if we can quickly eliminate him," Jonas said. "In fact, they'll probably be relieved when he's gone. I hated working for him, and I'm sure his followers' feelings against him have only increased."

"Then we just need to find a way to get rid of him that won't rile up his army against us," Mark said. "What are Sherem's weaknesses or fears?"

Jonas shook his head. "He doesn't have many. That's how he stays in control. There was only one time I only saw him really lose his composure. One of the warriors had brought a rattlesnake into the Capitol as a prank, and Sherem completely freaked out. He climbed onto the dining table until it had been killed and taken from the building. He hates snakes."

Tad's eyes grew wide, then he grinned widely. "I might have a solution for you."

He quickly told the others about his experience helping Mighty Tom feed his pet, and Jonas let out a whoop. "That could be perfect. Imagine how Sherem might react if he saw Tom's snake slithering toward him."

Mark frowned slightly. "Do you think Tom would let us use his pet in that way?"

"If Tom knows it would help get rid of Sherem, I think he'll be happy to help out," Tad said. "But I'm staying as far from that snake as I can."

# CHAPTER 24

Mark asked for Tom to be brought to the meeting room in the temple, and after the men had explained their plans to him about how to reclaim Salt Lake City, Tom was excited to be a part of it. As they explained Sammy's role in the plan, he felt confident the snake would be safe.

The men felt the need to keep their mission a secret from the other missionaries, because in order for their plan to work they had to keep their numbers small and not arouse suspicions among Sherem's followers. They did tell Tom's grandpa the plan just so somebody would know where they had gone, then that afternoon they slipped into the trucks and drove out of the temple compound.

They had taken a sturdy canvas tarp and fastened it tightly along the top edge of one of the truck beds, leaving a couple feet of clearance between the bed of the truck and the tarp—giving plenty of room to fit a 25-foot snake. As the sun began to set, the group pulled off the freeway near Thanksgiving Point in Lehi, where they discussed their plan a final time.

"Once it's completely dark, I'll lead the way and distract the guards at the Point of the Mountain," Jonas said. "Tad and Tom, once I radio to you that the coast is clear, you can follow me with Sammy in your truck. We should be able to make it to Temple Square without a problem, but Mark will remain here at Thanksgiving Point if we need any assistance. Sound good?"

The other men agreed, and they began an impatient wait for night to fall and the guards to likely be asleep. Finally at 11 p.m.

Jonas got into his truck and said to the others. "Wish me luck, and keep your radios on."

He traveled north on I-15, approaching the crest of the Point of the Mountain where the Utah County line once was. Thankfully the half-moon provided just enough light that he could keep his headlights off. He spotted a shack sitting directly in the middle of the freeway and figured it had to be where the guards were stationed. He turned off the engine and coasted to a stop fifty yards from the shack. He looked around cautiously for any sign of the guards, but he decided they must be inside sleeping.

Jonas quietly opened the truck door and crept forward with a box of matches and a bottle of lighter fluid. He soaked a corner of the shack with the fluid, then tossed a match at it. With a quiet "whoosh" the corner of the shack started to burn. It spread quickly, and soon the back wall of the shack was on fire, with flames licking the roof. He didn't want anyone to injured, but he hoped the guards would be disoriented enough that he could drive the truck past them without being noticed.

"Fire, fire!" he shouted, shaking the door before sprinting back to the truck. He started the engine and waited. Within seconds the door burst open and five men stumbled outside. They ran to the back of the building and tried to put out the flames, but it was already out of control.

The roar of the flames was surprisingly loud now, so Jonas decided to drive past them before they spotted him. He would come within a few yards of the shack, but there was no chance they'd stop him now. But before he could even roll forward, the guards moved away from the burning shack and after talking briefly among themselves, they fled into the darkness.

"What a bunch of cowards," Jonas said to himself. "I guess they don't want to face Sherem's wrath."

Jonas quickly radioed the others. "Well, that was easy. The guards took off into the hills already, so the road is clear to bring Sammy. I'll let you know if I see anything else, but otherwise I'll meet you at Temple Square."

✤ ✤ ✤

Just before midnight Jonas arrived in downtown Salt Lake City. He rolled to a stop on the south side of Temple Square near the Brigham Young statue. He stayed clear of the chainlink fence, remembering that it was electrified. He saw a guard half-asleep in a small security enclosure near the gate, so he turned off the truck and walked toward the enclosure. The man still didn't notice him, so he picked up some pebbles and threw them at the enclosure's window. The man inside jerked awake and peered outside at Jonas, but he seemed accustomed to such pestering and quickly ignored it. But Jonas kept popping the glass with pebbles until the man finally stood up and cracked the window open slightly.

"What do you want?" the man asked angrily.

"Hello, sir, my name is Jonas Ferguson, and I've come from New Jerusalem. I'm here to help liberate Salt Lake."

"All by yourself in the middle of the night?" the guard asked. "I think you've been hallucinating. Go away."

Jonas merely smiled. "No, the president of the Church sent me, and the key to our success is for you to let me into Temple Square. Then we can open the gate for another truck that will arrive in a few minutes."

The guard laughed. "That's a good one. Sherem's people have been trying all sorts of tricks to get in here, but that's the first time they've claimed to have been sent by the prophet."

Jonas was getting frustrated. "I'm completely serious. We know Sherem is afraid of snakes, and the truck is carrying a huge snake that is going to frighten him into surrendering."

That comment made the guard's ears perk up. He'd heard that old tale of Sherem freaking out over a rattlesnake. "Do you have any identification on you?" the guard asked.

"No, because part of our plan is to tell Sherem I have been held hostage by the Mormons for the past year . . . "

The guard's brief change of heart seemed to vanish. "Maybe I'm just really tired, but your story is sounding worse by the second."

Jonas stammered a little. "Sorry, but it's the truth."

He tried to figure out how he could convince the guard he wasn't an imposter. Then a name popped into his head.

"I'm friends with Doug Dalton," Jonas said. "He's been serving as one of the 144,000 high priests and he has just returned to New Jerusalem."

The guard did a quick double-take. "Doug Dalton! Now that's a name I know. He was one of my close friends growing up in Springville."

"So can you open the gate?" Jonas asked hopefully.

The guard thought for a moment. "Can you tell me anything else about the Daltons?"

"Sure. Doug's sister Emma married Tad North, and Doug's wife is named Becky. Tad will be in the truck that's coming here. You can ask him!"

"Very good," the guard said, suddenly feeling confident Jonas was telling the truth. But he had one more question. "What about their sister Lori?"

Jonas frowned. "I didn't know there was another child."

"There wasn't," the guard said with a smile. "I was just testing you. My name is Don Fowers. Let me turn off the electric fence so you can drive your truck inside."

❖ ❖ ❖

Soon Jonas and Don were standing near the gate watching carefully for the second truck to arrive. As they waited, Jonas shared with Don some of the details of their plan.

"I hope it works," Don said. "If we can get rid of Sherem, the people here will be civilized again. They've made a mess out of downtown, torn up several roads with their crazy chariot races, and cut down all of the trees."

"They sound like they stay busy," Jonas said.

"Actually, they're very lazy. They remind me of the Gadianton robbers. They don't really have a purpose in life without another group of people to fight against and steal from, and I think most of them are getting tired of it. I'll bet even Sherem's most loyal thugs would prefer a more productive lifestyle if they were given another option."

"Hopefully we'll be able to give that option soon," Jonas told him. "The trickiest part of the plan is that I need to make Sherem believe my story so I can gain his trust."

Jonas explained to Don about his past, including how he had been sent as a spy by Sherem to help destroy all of the Mormons living in Manti, but that in the end he'd chosen to warn them rather than get them all killed.

"So you were the one behind that?" Don asked. "We never knew quite how the Manti Saints knew they should leave."

"That was me," Jonas said. "I left Manti with the Saints and later joined the Church. Now I'm counting on the fact Sherem wouldn't have ever suspected I would defect. If he does, then I probably won't make it out alive."

"Well, I'll be praying for you," Don said. "I'd love to get Salt Lake back into the Church's hands. I have a lot of time to just sit her and ponder the future, and I really thought the Church might let Salt Lake stay under Sherem's control until the Second Coming."

Jonas smiled. "Let's just say Sherem's future is about to change."

# CHAPTER 25

About a half hour later the truck carrying Tad and Tom arrived at Temple Square's south gate, with Sammy tucked away in the truck bed. Don opened the gate, and they pulled the truck next to a set of doors on the south visitors center.

Don peeked under a corner of the tarp covering the truck bed and immediately leapt back. "Whoa! Snakes don't usually bother me, but this one is something else."

It took some persuasion, but Don finally let Tom take Sammy into a small room in the visitors center. Then the men had a restless night's sleep on some couches as they anticipated the events of the following day.

Jonas departed from Temple Square at sunrise and walked several blocks to the Capitol Building. He had changed into raggedy clothes, and Tad had smeared mud all over him to create the appearance he hadn't bathed in a long time. He felt confident that none of Sherem's followers knew what had really happened to him after he left their camp to go to Manti. The camp's leader, Ken Turner, might have eventually figured out that Jonas had betrayed them, but Richard Dalton had found Ken's body hanging from a tree near Birdseye.

As he walked up the Capitol steps, a man emerged from the shadows. "Stop right there," the man shouted.

Jonas halted and put his hands in the air. The man approached, and Jonas immediately recognized him. They had both been part of the army that had traveled to Manti. "Braxton, don't you recognize me?" Jonas said. "It's me, Jonas. The Mormons took me prisoner when I was sent as a spy to Manti, but I've finally been able to escape."

Braxton looked stunned. "We figured the Mormons had slit your throat."

Jonas frowned. "Well, they certainly treated me horribly. They took me all through the mountains and tried to get me to tell all of Sherem's secrets. But I never did crack."

"Do you think they'll try to recapture you?" Braxton asked.

Jonas shook his head. "They lost my trail a long time ago. I just wanted to get back here and let Sherem know what they're planning. Do you think he'll be willing to see me?"

"Absolutely."

Braxton took him to the main entrance and knocked on the door. After a few seconds it crept open. "What do you want?" a voice asked.

"An old friend has returned," Braxton said. The door opened wider, and Jonas saw another of his old acquaintances. He told his story again in greater detail, and the guard absorbed every word before eagerly escorting Jonas inside. "I know Sherem will be very interested to hear what you have to say."

Five minutes later Jonas found himself standing in front of twenty men who wanted to hear his story. Sherem then entered the room and actually gave him an awkward hug.

"It's such a relief to see you," Sherem said. "I knew in my heart that you'd been captured or killed by the Mormons, but there was always this nagging feeling about what really happened. I actually dreamed one night that they'd somehow converted you."

Jonas gave a nervous laugh. "Now *that* would be a story to tell, wouldn't it?"

As Sherem and the men laughed, Jonas quickly launched into the story he had concocted in his mind, including being held captive in one of the towers of the Manti Temple.

"I even saw our army outside the temple, but they had me bound and gagged. Then you all went away, and I knew my fate was sealed as a prisoner of the Mormons."

Braxton called out, "I'm so sorry, man! They had that electric fence turned on, and the place looked deserted. We would never have left if we'd known you were there."

"I know," Jonas said, strangely touched by Braxton's words. "That means a lot to hear you say that."

He spent the day listening to what Sherem's leaders had been doing during his absence, but there wasn't much variety in their stories. It really sounded like they had returned from Manti and then basically sat around since then.

By late afternoon, Jonas had bathed and shared an early dinner with Sherem—a tuna fish sandwich and a bowl of chicken noodle soup. Jonas sighed inwardly. This was the same meal he'd had last year at this very same table, except last time he'd also been served some soggy canned peas—they must have run out of them. But he kept a smile on his face and held up his glass of water toward Sherem. "My compliments to the chef. This food tastes great."

"Thank you," Sherem said. "Supplies are getting low, but at least we still have the good stuff."

Soon after the meal, Jonas feigned being exhausted. "I was on the run all night and I need to go to sleep, if that's all right," he told Sherem. "Then in the morning I can help pinpoint where the Mormons have been hiding in the mountains. They have a good supply of food, and I think we can finish them off."

"That would be wonderful," Sherem said. "The men have been itching for a fight, and they'd really enjoy that."

Jonas was given a cot to sleep on in a room on the main floor, and Sherem went upstairs to his spacious bedroom. Jonas lay anxiously on that cot for two hours, hoping everything was going fine with Tad and Tom.

At 11:30 p.m., he climbed off the cot and opened the Capitol's main door. The guard spun around and Jonas was pleased to see it was Braxton.

"Hey man, I'm so impressed you escaped from the Mormons," Braxton said. "It's so great to have you back."

"Yeah, everyone is treating me so well here."

"It's because you deserve it, man."

They talked for a minute more, then Jonas said, "You know what? I'd be happy to cover your assignment for a while if you wanted. I'm too hyped up to sleep, and I know you've had a long shift. You were on duty when I first got here!"

Braxton hesitated, but he couldn't see any harm in it. "Are you sure? I really could use a break."

"It would be my pleasure," Jonas said. "Feel free to go use my cot and shut the door. I'll come wake you up when I start feeling sleepy."

Braxton was grinning. "That would be awesome."

Within moments, Jonas found himself the lone guard at the front door to Sherem's castle. He knew the Lord had been assisting him all day, and getting Braxton out of the way was a huge help. But now he'd reached the point in the plan that hadn't been scripted. He set a lantern at his feet, hoping it would provide enough light for Tad and Tom to recognize him. He had butterflies in his stomach, knowing the next half hour might get a little tense.

Meanwhile, Tad had quietly driven their truck up the hill once darkness had settled in. It was a little difficult with the headlights turned off, but soon they were close enough to see the front door of the Capitol. He knew it was a gamble to drive so close, but he decided if Jonas hadn't been able to convince Sherem he'd been held captive by the Mormons, there would've been a lot more activity going on throughout the city. Instead, it was quiet, so it gave him hope that Jonas had succeeded.

Tad and Tom decided to wait until midnight before moving closer. That was the time Jonas had hoped to somehow get the front door open for them.

As they waited, Tom checked on Sammy. "How's he doing?" Tad asked when he returned to the truck cab.

"Fine," Tom responded. "He certainly isn't hungry. I shouldn't have fed him that half a deer a couple days ago."

Tad laughed. "We don't want him to eat Sherem, just scare him to death."

At five minutes to midnight, Tad grabbed a pair of binoculars Tom had brought along. He focused on the guard at the front door, then passed the binoculars to Tom. "Does that look like Jonas to you?"

Tom took his turn with the binoculars, and then nodded. "I think it is! He sure seems to be looking intently in our direction."

Tad turned on the engine and put his hand on the headlight switch. He held his breath as he quickly switched the lights on and off. They were on for only a split second, but they caught the attention of the guard, who suddenly started motioning to them.

"What do you think?" Tad asked. "Does he want us to drive up there?"

The guard then started jumping up and down, waving his arms above his head.

"I think so."

Tad drove slowly up the road, and it became clear that the guard was indeed Jonas, who motioned for him to back the truck up to the steps. As soon as the back tires hit the steps, Tad turned off the truck, and Tom jumped out to let down the tailgate. As Sammy's massive head emerged from the back of the truck, Tom slipped a rope over his head and led him up the steps. Jonas was waiting at the door.

"We need to act fast," Jonas said, nearly hyperventilating. "Sherem is asleep in a room at the top of the rotunda's stairs. We might need to break down the door, but then we'll let Sammy loose and let him do his work."

Jonas threw the front door open, and the three men rushed up the stairs, closely followed by a monstrous snake.

Sherem sat up in bed and listened closely. It sounded like there were people climbing the stairs.

"I need my peace and quiet," he muttered to himself. He left his bed, marched across the room and flung open the door, finding himself face-to-face with Sammy.

Sherem stopped literally in mid-step, petrified by what he saw before him. Sammy slowly slithered closer until Sherem finally came to his senses and began running away. A strangled scream escaped his throat as he tried to climb onto a chest of drawers. Sammy thought this was all a game and happily followed along, moving forward to receive a pat on the head.

Sherem let out another shriek and then jumped to a window ledge, pushing hard against the window. In his frenzy, he had forgotten he was on the third floor, and by the time he realized it, he was halfway out the window. He tried to scramble back into the room, only to find Sammy's face six inches from his. Sammy's tongue flicked out, catching Sherem on the cheek, and that was all it took for Sherem to leap backward in terror.

Tom rushed into the room to take hold of the rope around Sammy's head and pull him away from the window, and Jonas rushed to the open window to see the outcome. It wasn't pretty. Sherem lay motionless on a concrete walkway with his limbs horribly twisted. Jonas turned away, feeling a little sick. Their mission was complete, but he always hated to see someone die, even a person as evil as Sherem.

Tad had stayed at the bedroom door as a lookout. As Tom brought Sammy back to the doorway, he said, "I haven't seen anyone. Let's get out of here."

Within a minute, the three men had reached the truck, but Tom couldn't get Sammy to cooperate. He had been cooped up for too long and squirmed away from Tom's efforts to get him into the truck bed.

Finally Tom said, "Tad, you go ahead and drive down to Temple Square. I guess I'll just give Sammy some fresh air."

"Okay, I'll be waiting for you there."

Jonas moved back up the stairs and said, "Great job, but I better stay here and see what happens. If I suddenly disappear again, I'm pretty sure who would get the blame."

As Tad drove the truck away, Tom led Sammy down the hill. The incident with Sherem had happened so fast that he still couldn't quite comprehend it. His pet snake was an unsung hero.

Once Tom got Sammy back to Temple Square and found Tad, the snake was a bit more worn out, and Tom was able to coax him into the truck. Even though it was now 1 a.m., Tad and Tom felt it would be best to get Sammy safely out of the Salt Lake Valley and back to the Bean Museum as soon as possible. They still weren't sure how Sherem's men were going to react to his death, and it would be best to have the snake out of the way. They had a feeling Jonas would be able to take care of himself.

Jonas slowly walked back to his post at the front door. He was amazed that none of the other men had awakened, but in reality the entire episode had been done in silence, other than Sherem's brief terrified screams.

The entire building was now dark, other than his lantern on the front steps. He went inside the building to his room and woke up Braxton, who sat up groggily.

"I think I'm ready to go to sleep now," Jonas told him.

Braxton yawned. "Hey, thanks for letting me rest. I really needed it."

"It was my pleasure. See you in the morning."

To his surprise, Jonas did sleep quite well. He was awakened several hours later by a lot of shouting. He left his room and went outside where several men were standing over Sherem's body.

"What happened?" he asked one of the men.

"It's hard to believe, but it looks like Sherem committed suicide by jumping from his bedroom window."

Jonas shook his head sorrowfully. "What a shame. I hope the Mormons don't hear about this."

The man looked alarmed. "What do you mean?"

"I think they might attack us if they know Sherem is dead. I don't know about you, but I'm heading for the mountains."

"Good idea," the man said, and he then turned to the man next to him and conveyed the same fears. Jonas watched as each of these supposedly loyal men took a final glance at Sherem and then slipped away, just as Jonas had hoped. After five minutes, he was alone with Sherem's body. Jonas looked into the air above the body and said aloud, "I'm sure you're still here in spirit, Sherem. Was it all worth it?"

Jonas returned inside briefly to find a blanket and a shovel. Then he returned and wrapped the body in the blanket before digging a shallow grave in a nearby flower garden. He lowered the body in the hole and quickly filled the grave with dirt. As he scooped the last bit of soil over Sherem's remains, he said, "Good riddance, Larry Campbell. I've taken care of your body. Now go meet your master. I'm sure he's eager to bind you in his chains."

Jonas stopped at Temple Square to tell Don Fowers and the other missionaries what had happened, including that Sherem's most loyal men had fled into the mountains. The guards rejoiced and congratulated him.

"That's wonderful," Don said. "Now we can finally turn Salt Lake into a city of Zion."

Jonas then climbed into his truck and drove through other sections of the city, telling anyone he saw that Sherem was dead and that the Mormons would be coming soon to bring civilization back to the valley. Most of the people were happy with the news, while a few decided they better depart as quickly as possible.

Jonas drove back to the Provo Temple that afternoon and had a good meeting with Mark Dalton, who said the First Presidency had been notified of Sherem's death. They were already planning to issue calls to groups of Saints living in small Zion communities in Idaho and northern Utah to move to Salt Lake. The city would be revitalized within weeks. Jonas, Tad, and Mark were eager to return to New Jerusalem, and they invited Angie and Tom to join them. She seemed interested, but Tom shook his head.

"Not yet," he said. "I want to stay with my grandpa for a while longer. Besides, I can't just leave my pets."

The men nodded, and then Tom looked across the temple grounds at the column of smoke rising from across the lake. He smiled slightly and added, "And you know what? I feel like I need to preach the gospel to the kids living in Lincoln Point. Like I said before, I think they just need someone to give them some direction in life."

# CHAPTER 26

Halfway around the world, Mitko Petrov stood in the shadows of Moscow's Red Square. He had spent many years in Bulgaria, and Moscow had always been the city everyone admired from afar. Yet it was also the symbol of everything that had gone wrong in their country. Communism had created many difficulties—or cost the lives—of many of Mitko's relatives during the past century.

When the Russian revolutionary Vladimir Lenin moved the Soviet government from Petrograd to Moscow in 1918, he selected the historic fortified complex known as the Kremlin as his home, and it still served as the official residence of the President of Russia. Now Mitko stood outside its walls, and from the information he had gathered through conversations with Russia's citizens during his journey from Siberia, some of the most vile and heartless men on the planet were now living inside the Kremlin—the leaders of the Coalition forces. These men had sought to destroy the United States, and now they were actively recruiting soldiers to become part of their latest wicked plan to conquer the world.

Mitko walked toward a clothing shop on the square and looked into the reflection of a window pane. He hardly recognized himself. Ever since saying goodbye to Elder Brown in Siberia several weeks earlier, Mitko had let his hair grow into a shaggy mess, and he'd also grown a thick beard. His clothes had become tattered, and he had lost nearly 30 pounds. It was true that he'd been quite hungry during portions on his journey, but he also wanted to "look the part" if he found a way to meet with the Coalition leaders.

He had rehearsed his story well. Over and over during his

journey he told people he had been a part of the Coalition forces that attacked America, but that in the end they had been defeated by the Americans. He had escaped from them and was now traveling around the world to tell the Coalition leaders what had happened there.

His story had gained him a lot of sympathy along the way—including rides in the back of trucks, free meals, and barns to sleep in. During his journey he realized once again what good-hearted souls the Russian people were. These world wars hadn't been caused by the common people, but rather by government leaders seeking power and wealth.

Elder Brown hadn't given him any instructions about what to do once he arrived in Moscow. He felt a lot like Nephi did when he had been sent back to retrieve the brass plates from Laban—he was simply trusting the Spirit to guide him.

Overall, Mitko had been able to get a good idea through the public grapevine of what was happening within the Coalition. In the past few weeks, Russia and China had ended their foolish border dispute and were working together again. Their defeat in America—combined with their own squabbles—had left their armies depleted, but there were still millions of men willing to serve in the Coalition armies.

As their armies began to take shape once again, an alliance was formed with several Islamic countries, with Iran leading the way. Iran's president, who had been in office since even before the fall of the United States, had often spoken publicly about his disdain for the Jewish people. Now he was using his influence to proclaim that an attack on Israel would be a wonderful military exercise.

The Iranian leader's hatred for the Jewish state was somewhat irrational and based on long-standing false beliefs, but Satan and his minions had been whispering in his ears for many years that the Jews deserved to be destroyed. Now he was seeking to make those ideas a reality.

✣ ✣ ✣

Mitko knew he couldn't stand around much longer in Red Square without attracting unwanted attention, so he prayed fervently for the gift of tongues to help out his limited knowledge of the Russian language. He then cautiously approached a well-guarded entrance into the Kremlin. He began speaking hastily in rudimentary Russian, "Help me! I fought in the war against America and I'm one of the few survivors. I've traveled around the world to tell the leaders what I know."

The guard stared at him, hardly believing what he was hearing. He looked at the ill-kept man before him and nearly discounted him as a drunken stooge, but something in Mitko's eyes made the guard reconsider. He had never heard of a Coalition soldier returning to Russia, so that in itself was intriguing.

The guard pondered for a moment, and figured if he let him in, he'd be out of his hair either way. If the leaders felt this man was lying, they would have him killed or imprisoned. Of course, on the slim chance the man was telling the truth, the guard knew it was of utmost importance to the leaders and he might be rewarded for notifying them.

"Step inside," the guard told Mitko.

He first gave Mitko an uncomfortable strip search and then led him to another checkpoint, where Mitko told his story once again. After a few minutes, he advanced farther into the Kremlin, and soon stood outside the entrance to the main assembly room of the Coalition leaders. Several leaders were milling around, waiting for their next meeting to start shortly. A note about Mitko had been passed to the Russian prime minister, who had been in power even longer than his Iranian colleague. The Russian read it twice, hardly believing it. Then he looked to the hallway and saw Mitko's disheveled frame.

"Keep him there," the Russian said. "We'll talk to him during the meeting."

Mitko continued to pray for help with the language as he waited to speak with the leaders. He knew it was a miracle he had even made it this far into the Kremlin.

The meeting started, and about a dozen men gathered around a table to discuss their upcoming plans. After about twenty minutes, the Russian pointed to the hallway and motioned for the guard to escort Mitko to the center of the room. The Russian then explained Mitko's claims, and the men perked right up.

The Russian asked Mitko to tell his story, and he gave the leaders a detailed description of the final battle in Denver. The leaders asked him many questions, and he was surprised to learn that the leaders hadn't ever been sure of what had actually happened to the remaining Coalition soldiers. The final report they had received indicated the remaining soldiers were marching to occupy cities in the Rocky Mountains. Their commanding officers hadn't mentioned encountering any opposition—and then the reports suddenly stopped, as if the Coalition army had dropped off the face of the earth.

The leaders had feared the army had been struck down by a resurgence of the flu-like virus that had killed many of their soldiers during the harsh winter. They had never even considered that the Americans had actually defeated their men. Anger filled the faces of the leaders as Mitko told how the Americans had led the Coalition forces into a trap at Mile High Stadium.

"What fools our soldiers were," the Russian prime minister said, his face growing red. "They deserved to be ambushed. Are the Americans still there?"

"Yes, and they are very powerful," Mitko said. "I wouldn't attack them again."

The Iranian raised his voice. "Forget the Americans. We can defeat them after we have crushed the maggots in Jerusalem."

The leaders seemed to believe Mitko's story, but to his surprise, he was soon dismissed and taken directly to an isolated jail cell in another part of the Kremlin. As the guard locked the cell, Mitko asked, "Why am I in here? I told them the truth."

The guard nodded, seeming to understand his feelings. "I

know, but they never trust anybody. In a few days, they'll bring you back into another meeting and see if your story has changed. So I wouldn't change it, whether what you said is true or not."

The guard locked the cell, and Mitko sat in silence. There wasn't another prisoner in his section, and he felt abandoned. "What is my purpose here?" he thought. "Am I just going to rot in jail for several months?"

Each day he made sure to be extremely pleasant to the jailer who brought him his meals each day. He hoped it would pay off. After a week, Mitko asked him for a favor. "Could I get a pen and a piece of paper?"

"What for?" the guard asked.

"I just want to write a letter to a friend. I know it will never be delivered, but at least I will have written it."

The guard looked around. "I really shouldn't give you anything, but I can slip it onto the tray of your next meal."

"Thank you so much."

As Mitko waited for his next meal to arrive, he composed the letter in his head. When the pen and paper arrived as promised, he hurriedly wrote the letter. When he was finished, he folded it carefully and knelt down to pray.

"Heavenly Father, I think I understand why I'm here. I've written a message to the prophet, and I feel the only way I can have it delivered is by thy servant John. Please send him here so I can give him the letter."

A few minutes later Mitko heard the door of the enclosure open, and he was elated to see John walk in.

"Thank goodness you're here," Mitko said. "I was afraid I was going to have to eat my letter if the guards came back."

John smiled. "We wouldn't want that."

Mitko suddenly had an idea. "Can't you just set me free? I'm ready to go back to Zion now."

John shook his head. "Your work here is far from finished. But I'll be happy to take your letter and help get everything in motion back in New Jerusalem."

Mitko was thoughtful. "So you know how this is going to end up, don't you?"

John looked a little puzzled, and then Mitko suddenly felt a bit silly. He was asking a translated being—and the man who wrote the Book of Revelation—if he knew what was going to happen.

John reached both of his hands through the cell bars and clasped Mitko's shoulders. "Yes, I do know what is going to happen, and it won't necessarily be easy. Just follow the promptings of the Holy Ghost and things will work out for you as the Lord has designed."

Mitko nodded. "That's about all I can do right now."

"Well, give me the letter and I'll be on my way to see the prophet," John said. "By the way, the Ten Tribes are safely in New Jerusalem, so Zion is growing by leaps and bounds."

"I'm glad to hear that."

"Be strong, Mitko," John said. "Don't forget this is only for a small moment, and then you'll gain your eternal reward."

Then John took the letter, stuck it in his pocket, and with a small wave good-bye, exited the enclosure.

Once he was gone, Mitko sat on his metal bed, feeling like the world was crushing down on him. He had really hoped John would help him escape, but John had made it clear that there were additional reasons for him to be inside the Kremlin. He just hoped he had the inner strength to interact effectively with those evil men when the time came.

# CHAPTER 27

❧

Within a few minutes, the prophet was holding the letter Mitko had given to John. He opened it up and was alarmed by the contents. It read:

*Dear First Presidency:*

*This is from Mitko Petrov. I have reached the Kremlin, and I was interviewed by the leaders of the Coalition. They believe I'm a Coalition soldier who has miraculously made my way back to Moscow. I told them how the Coalition forces had been defeated, and I warned them that the Americans now had a strong army, so hopefully they will postpone another attack on America, although it is clearly in their long-range plans.*

*However, why I am writing this letter is because the Coalition is regrouping quickly, and they have added several Islamic countries to their ranks. The most outspoken among them is the Iranian leader. He clearly hates the Jews, and he is determined to destroy Israel first, before they attack any other country.*

*You certainly understand my worry about that. It seems that the pieces are falling into place for the prophecies to be fulfilled concerning the battle of Armageddon, where a huge army from the north will attack Israel. The only reason Israel will survive is through the acts and miracles of two latter-day prophets. As far as I know, those prophets aren't in Jerusalem yet.*

*I am currently locked in a jail cell, but I think the leaders trust me, and I expect to be here for a while longer. Hopefully I'll be able to relay to you any additional information I discover concerning the Coalition's plans, but I really feel that something must be done to protect Israel.*

*The Coalition leaders haven't set a timetable yet, because they are still assembling and training a new group of soldiers, but I expect the attack will come within a few weeks.*

*Pray for me.*

*Mitko Petrov*

The prophet folded the letter and opened his scriptures to Section 77 in the Doctrine and Covenants. He'd read the entire section recently where the Lord answers some of Joseph Smith's questions concerning the Book of Revelation, but now he focused in on verse 15. He read it aloud slowly, making sure he didn't miss anything.

"*Q. What is to be understood by the two witnesses, in the eleventh chapter of Revelation?*

"*A. They are two prophets that are to be raised up to the Jewish nation in the last days, at the time of the restoration, and to prophesy to the Jews after they are gathered and have built the city of Jerusalem in the land of their forefathers.*"

The prophet sat back. The Jews had indeed gathered to Jerusalem in the past century, and after the nation of Israel was established in 1948, they had built a beautiful city that was the envy of other nations. All of the outside factors in the prophecy had been fulfilled.

The prophet stood from his desk and walked directly to a sacred room in the temple called the Holy of Holies where he could contemplate the needs of the Church and receive the answers he needed. After kneeling in prayer for several minutes, pleading to Heavenly Father for guidance, a familiar light appeared at the end of the room, and the Lord Jesus Christ stood before him.

The prophet bowed before him and said, "After reading Mitko Petrov's letter, I feel the time has come to send the two prophets to Jerusalem."

"That is right," the Lord responded.

The prophet paused, making sure he worded his statements

correctly. When he first became the prophet, he would ask Jesus questions, but the Lord would simply ask a question back, forcing him to make a choice. So the prophet soon realized the best way to get an answer was to make a wise, informed decision and then confirm it with the Lord.

The prophet cleared his throat and said, "I have come to understand that these two prophets will be selected from our current First Presidency and Twelve Apostles."

"Correct," the Lord said.

"As I have studied the Book of Revelation, I realize this assignment will be among the most difficult any apostle could has receive. It will require men who possess a mixture of physical strength, emotional stability, and spiritual power. As I have carefully evaluated the fourteen apostles—fifteen counting myself, I suppose—I have narrowed it down to four men. The others are either too old, frail or ill to endure such a lengthy and challenging assignment. After all, we can't afford to have one of them die on us over there."

The Lord appreciated the prophet's attempt to lighten the mood as they discussed the matter, and he gave a soft laugh. "Yes, we need them to serve for the duration of the assignment."

The prophet stood and began pacing around the room. "All four men would do an excellent job. The problem is that my heart is trying to overrule my head. Two of them have little children who wouldn't see their fathers for more than three years. And their dear wives have already been through so much . . ."

"I understand," the Lord said, "but I will watch over and bless their families."

The prophet nodded. "So after much pondering and prayer, the Holy Ghost has confirmed to me that Elder Joshua Brown and Elder Colton Negus are the two apostles who must be sent to Jerusalem immediately."

"That is the right decision," the Lord said.

The prophet gave a sigh of relief, and the Lord stepped forward, radiating purity and righteousness. He put his arm around the prophet's shoulder and said, "Thank you for carrying such a heavy burden. I know the difficult choices seem to never end. I assure you, however, the time is not far off when I will usher in the great millennial era, and we will live in peace and harmony."

The prophet smiled up at the Savior. "I know the end is approaching. The Saints will be ready."

# APPROACHING THE FINAL HOURS

———— ⚜ ————

As Zion has risen to great heights, the Second Coming seems imminent, but several crucial events remain to be completed. Among these are:

The defense of Jerusalem by the two apostles against the Coalition armies led by Gog and Magog.

The continuation of Mitko Petrov's dangerous mission among the Coalition leaders.

The great meeting held in the Valley of Adam-ondi-Ahman, where the prophets from each dispensation will be gathered to return the priesthood keys of the kingdom to the Savior.

Meanwhile, the veil will continue to grow thinner between the Saints on earth and those in Spirit World as temple work flourishes.

Read about these events and many others as the *Standing in Holy Places* series continues in *Book Four: The Keys of the Kingdom.*

# About the Author

———— ⚜ ————

Chad Daybell has worked in the publishing business for the past two decades and has written more than 20 books.

The first two books in this series—*The Great Gathering* and *The Celestial City*—have become bestsellers in both the LDS bookstores and the national retail chains.

Chad is also known for his other novels such as *Chasing Paradise* and *The Emma Trilogy*, as well as his non-fiction books for youth, including *The Aaronic Priesthood* and *The Youth of Zion*. He and his wife Tammy also created the *Tiny Talks* series for Primary children.

Learn about Chad and the upcoming volumes in the *Standing in Holy Places* series at his personal website **www.cdaybell.com**.